RECONSTRUCTING COMPETITION AND ITS PROCESSES

A abstract idea that leads to reconstructing and giving a sharper focus to competitive strategy

Baisham Chatterjee

iUniverse, Inc.
New York Bloomington

Reconstructing competition and its processes
A abstract idea that leads to reconstructing and giving a sharper focus to competitive strategy

iUniverse books may be ordered through booksellers or by contacting:

iUniverse
1663 Liberty Drive
Bloomington, IN 47403
www.iuniverse.com
1-800-Authors (1-800-288-4677)

Because of the dynamic nature of the Internet, any Web addresses or links contained in this book may have changed since publication and may no longer be valid. The views expressed in this work are solely those of the author and do not necessarily reflect the views of the publisher, and the publisher hereby disclaims any responsibility for them.

ISBN: 978-1-4401-6918-2 (pbk)
ISBN: 978-1-4401-6919-9 (ebook)

Printed in the United States of America

iUniverse rev. date:8/25/09

AUTHOR BIOGRAPHY

I gained my expertise around 3 years back from a very challenging project at Philips Analytical (Spectris Technologies) and then some experience in a German firm where I had played certain leadership role. Then came my very amazing blog http://baisham.blogspot.com/ which I created from my thoughts from HBS books and articles and of course my friends in Europe told that it had exemplary thought process. I have also written a few papers on E-commerce, corporate strategy and HR after I took admission at UNBSJ around 9 months back. I also contribute regularly or whenever I have time in the comments section of Ivey Business Journal articles. I also keep on blogging at ideablob.com as mf66. I stay in Saint John, NB, Canada and I have always been a voracious reader .

ACKNOWLEDGEMENTS

I thank my guide Gregory J. Fleet for being able to contribute earlier in paper writing and some project research. I also thank Mark Hollingworth (Prof McGill University) for appreciating me and encouraging me sometimes. I also thank Meredith Joy Henry for having helped me in certain critical situations and understood them. I also thank Donna McDermott for having helped me with the banking transactions. I also thank Jana Comeau for given me the opportunity to write papers on E-commerce for her. I also thank Bonnie Sudul. I also thank my friend Roger Moser for having come to know from him that I have to contribute. I also thank John Potts and Sarah Wilkinson of i.Universe for having helped me to write this book.

Lastly I thank the Ward Chipman library at UNBSJ for having derived all the data and references from the library.

PREFACE AND INTRODUCTION

This book leaves the idea behind the major forces of contribution in modern competitive strategy. I named my book **Reconstructing competition and its processes** based on the major facts that are the key functional forces of modern competition. I have discussed a lot about product innovation processes, economy and technology management that indeed help competition. Probably the identified processes are the key factors that drive growth stage and most of the ideas considered possess a key idea in developing modern business sense. This book consists of very old ideas being modernized and reconstructed to give a new shape to those previously vague processes and future situations.

Chapter 1 describes how start up companies and high tech firms are re-inventing new ideas and procedures for start up firms and assessing the innovation skills in creative businesses that undermines the competitive attitude of firms through its development in international markets. It is very necessary to specify CRM, cost structure patterns in emotionally oriented businesses. After that a business cycle and a high growth specification model has been determined.

Chapter 2 discusses various new product development ideas starting from demand analysis and its techniques for certain circumstances. Moreover a forecast has also been made along with technology-economy performance measures. Moreover an outlook has been created based on research intensive and development intensive comparison and frameworking. I have also talked in detail about market opportunity and R&D opportunities that can create very important yet very sustainable products that can stay more in the maturity stage. A view from the earlier RAND Corporation strategies has been made broader. A lot more in detail.

Chapter 3 describes product pitfalls and the steps that can be taken to reduce these pitfalls moreover there is description of buyers costs assigned to these pitfalls. Moreover there is a discussion on fluctuations. Moreover there has been more of a discussion on product creation stage. After that there has been certain discussed views on plant environment, market environment and scientific environment. Ideas has also been provided on typical marketing decision and product maturity. Different ideas on supply and distribution has also been developed.

Chapter 4 describes the economic scenario that can help businesses grow more challenging in different economies and the necessary requirements and the transitions, phases and different economic and market criteria the firm has to go through to reach this stage.

Chapter 5 draws the idea of the different factors of synergy on ROI, the different aspects of diversified firms, shared alignments and the different operating benefits. Other terms used are networking for synergy, different operating processes. Other terms talked of are strategic leadership, strategic architecture processes. Other factors talked of are different competences.

Chapter 6 states many examples that helps in correlating economics to innovation using financial strategies and advanced technology. International competition is another key area to concentrate on with allocative efficiency and productive efficiency. Moreover international competition improves the cost and efficiency levels of individual firms. Other key areas to talk of are innovator regimes, challenge world markets face and its approaches. As well as R&D capacity and capability.

Chapter 7 draws a major impact by using the value chain to implement value proposition, cost minimization, organization structure. Other factors talked of are technological linkage, core processes and the various opportunities and the contributive ability that the value chain can provide.

Chapter 8 describes the breakthrough in decision making where the most challenging breakthrough decision making has been talked of which can create useful profit potentiality, diversification by analyzing equipment needs. Other things talked of are long term planning and success and failure of long term planning. Other things involved are grapevine program. A lot more in detail.

Chapter 9 gives the idea of developing business in target segments by satisfying customers needs. Other things talked of are idea managers that create the major impact on competitive strategy. A CRM and a SWOT analysis is very important.

Chapter 10 looks forward towards changing technology and business prospects with threats from emerging nations. The case of emergence of a new market segment as well as risk factors has also been determined. Other factors talked of are linkages, changing pattern. Changing productivity, upgradation program. Other things talked of are productivity and the definition of the business cycle in strata 1, strata2 and strata 3 is very important.

Chapter 11 gives the clear description as to where technology should go taking the case of sustainable strategy and what are the strategies that the firm can take up to develop to reduce carbon emission, develop products that create impacts without the use of steel and create products that don't fail. A lot more of ideas.

Baisham Chatterjee

The conclusion gives the in depth discussion of what the book and the authors perception can bring together.

CONTENTS

Chapter 1

Perceiving Competition in High Growth Economy

By: Baisham Chatterjee (student UNBSJ)

The high level of competition is arising in the emerging markets where most of the developed and other developing nations are taking steps to maximize their market share and revenues. Today, companies evolving with new ideas generally have the most advanced demand for the strategic brand image as well as their services and product through unique entrepreneurship.

Countries like China are creating emerging areas of competitiveness in a different way like making technology invented by the western world more relevant in their perspective and then making the most use of it (re-inventing). However, companies that come up with new ideas, create new markets and target uncontested market space can make competition irrelevant. It is generally old businesses that change competitive rules by diverging to new areas of growth and better prospects. During a high growth stage in an economy, production companies always look for alternative source of production technology to grow further and possess a serious challenge to their competitors who have diversified to similar business, but it is more uncertain for small companies or start-up firms to have multiple sources of technology[1].

Relating to this the aspects that are to be studied are:

i) Industry condition of competing firms and characteristics of customers.
ii) Start- up companies have difficulty for accessing distribution channels but if a start up firm thinks of something unique, it can build certain alliances

with mid size firms. Example: A construction firm can share the market expansion strategy and competitive strategy with a steel industry to capture emerging segments like high-tech cities having most advanced infrastructure and also move into areas where their uses are similar.

iii) It is obvious that there are competitive and technological uncertainties and hence start ups should create a customer database and effectively build a target market strategy and make an idea of emerging application of the product in the segment in which it would be most effective.

iv) Start up firms need proper retraining of employees mainly through a HR consulting specialist in that area.

v) The circumstances in different foreign markets are different, roles of foreign government is different as well as the cost factor in different countries is different. Hence startups with the most unique technology should be exporting their products or services abroad and hence they should be able to understand the difference in resources and competitive attitude of firms in that country by analyzing international markets through previous experience. It is also necessary to focus on competitive ideas in that particular segment in a worldwide perspective.

As a firm grows larger, it should reconstruct market boundaries and look at the bigger picture of the global market scenario. Factors of success in immense competition are:

vi) Do something new to stand out of the strategic group these competing companies play in [2].

vii) At first a firm should focus in same purchasers or users but more over give more importance to using CRM to formulate strategy and look at the competitive threat in formulating that strategy.

Firms should go for creating products with the most exceptional value that do not miss the commonalities valued by mass of people rather than going for most sophisticated technology.

A Hungarian bus company NABI gained 20% of the market share throughout the world with its fiber glass buses that would lead to corrosion prevention, lesser fuel consumption and easier maintenance. Their thought as it is more scientific, may reduce competition and make them market leaders after a span of 20 years.

Even a vacuum cleaner can be so designed as done by Dyson to avoid the cost of purchase of vacuum cleaner bags as there would be no need to change it [1].

Understanding the implications underlying this sort of competitive advantage, it definitely takes one company ahead of other competitors. Cost structure patterns, lower inventory costs and most efficient process can also bring in competitive advantage.

Emotionally oriented businesses i.e. mainly big businesses that rise from nowhere and existing through personal relationship in the verge of becoming market leaders can be transformed in to low cost high performance businesses. In the modern era of 21st century businesses should run in such a way that there is exceptional buyer utility through value creation and performance, turning the product into a low cost product so that maximum customers can afford it.

Comparative as well as competitive pricing based on buyer cost and segmentation should be given importance so that an increasing amount of profit is attained on the year wise basis. Similarly to adopt this idea in a high growth economy the risk factor, uncertainty of organizations during high growth stage as well as production gap should be analyzed to bring in latest managerial thoughts and innovate new product for smoother production through advanced research. Business can be transformed in high growth economy through analysis of all the present factors that affect competition as well as its future factors [3].

Business transformation model in high growth economy for making competition irrelevant through turn around strategy

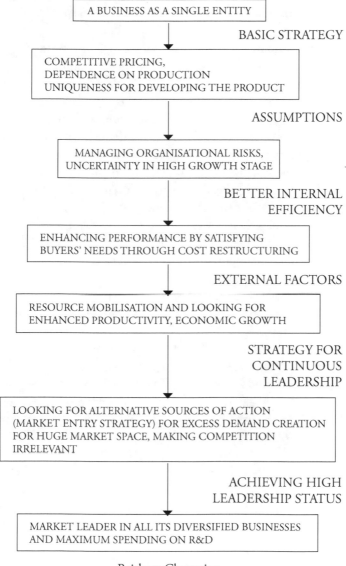

Baisham Chatterjee

High growth firms and economies can use a continuous idea of target market mix i.e. 4Ps to gather all kinds of ideas to forecast the market as well as create a major strategic and business re innovation through joint research and licensing agreements.

Joint research narrows the gap to a firm's productivity through innovation and the actual market scenario.

Joint research reduces the cost and risk of entering new businesses with the product in markets by bringing in to action the thought process of innovation, which would be more customer friendly, reliable, easily understandable, having better looks of the product, their place of production and brand name suitable to be launched in the market [4].

Sales promotion can create valued customers which can create a change in competitive attitude and CRM tactics.

Joint research helps in generalized marketing as well as niche marketing by understanding the market boundaries and demographic segmentation. It also creates market strength by creating new products for existing markets. Competition should be so well forecasted so that new entrants cannot bring new capacity and seek market share from moderate future leader by pushing down margins which would lead to price cutting. Instead there should be a little more spending on R&D. In a high growth economy, competition is intense from all aspects both domestically and from international firms [5].

Increasing patents through a well defined and intense R&D investment can lessen competition and reduce after-sales-service cost.

A cycle for understanding the competitive scenario in high growth economies
(with constant change in ideas)

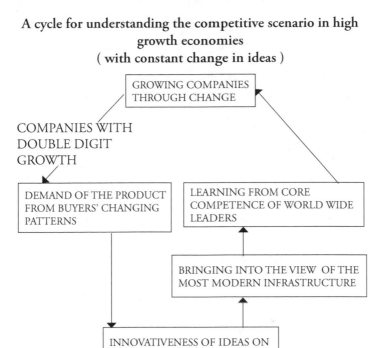

Baisham Chatterjee

Hence to grow further in growing economies the core competence, emerging industry segments, shifting buyers' needs, government regulations, patterns of trade and development and other macro and micro factors have to be studied. Very often competition is based on the different aspects of the value chain. Technology integration is a very big factor. And to bring about interconnection the business should think of collaboration that would interconnect different departments through a proper linkage. A broad focus on future competition comes from businesses that can forecast and exploit its self competencies and relate and understand that to the situation and competitive edge in other countries.

Very often the competitive edge shifts. Sometimes it seems that mergers and acquisitions stand as a key factor. But at certain time the proper economic system and markets have to be focused on to make it happen. Nothing should get affected through this. Very often certain economic factors disrupt probable situations which can make it difficult to build up on sustainable strategies which is a very important phenomenon to deal with in the future.

Very often it becomes difficult to adopt to changes and threat from BRIC nations this is when businesses in countries with a backlog in manufacturing should look at its global networks and procurement to succeed.

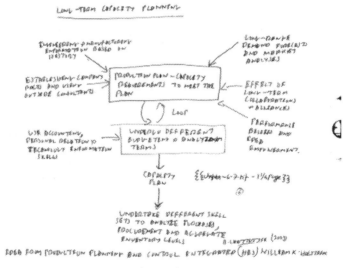

Baisham Chatterjee

Chapter 2

Competitive advantage involved in new product development and idea generation

By: Baisham Chatterjee (student UNBSJ)

If a new product is developed with a patentable invention and is such that another company might readily imitate it for manufacture and sale in other countries and might even sell it in the US then the US patent rights can verify before it is sold over there, if the patent is copied. But in many cases in this open market economy restrictions have been reduced a lot.

Technology is a knowledge of physical relationships that can range from the initial glimmerings of how a basic phenomenon can be applied to the solution of a practical problem to an end product, device or production machine in a mature operating system. In the conditional demand analysis shale oil recovery techniques will be required under any of the several circumstances-

➢ If shale oil mining, restoring, and transportation costs can be reduced so that shale crude at the refinery costs less than other crude sources. This is a very competitive process and can be done through the logistics requirements in the middle and how fast all these three can be joined.

➢ If foreign crude supplies are severely curtailed. Ex- it is a question of resource availability or efficiency of a firm to search for other resources and implement faster management processes and other tactics.

➢ If shale oil permits the refinery to produce an output mix of sufficiently greater value than other hydrocarbon sources. It is location that matters the most in this factor and ability to sell and get new customers.

➢ If international hydrocarbon finding, lifting and transportation costs exceed certain levels.

➢ If pegged international crude prices become too high.

The final forecast can predict:

➢ Whether there is a strong enough need to justify seeking some form of technical solution. It is very important to note the availability of new technologies required to evolve management techniques, that would automatically help in developing better production processes.

➢ The performance requirements any solution must meet if it is to be successful under various conditions.

➢ How rapidly present technical advances and the vulnerability of anticipated roadblocks indicate that shale can substitute for other resources under specific circumstances.

➢ The probability of each circumstance occurring by some future date. A future date of new news broadcasts, future sources and latest comments on environmental challenges that the firm may be ready to face are certain circumstances needed to be reacted to.

➢ The payoff in the event occurs and if the state of art is as anticipated.

Many years back a firm known as RAND Corporation first undertook the trends in plotting technical-economic performance.

> ➤ An analysis was made between large underground superhighway and parking complexes are becoming economically feasible and aesthetically attractive alternatives to conventional superhighways in dense urban areas. The study of the cost factor in constructing and building underground superhighways with same capacity has become an important area of study.

In such trend analysis important problems are recognized:

> ➤ Data can be derived from sparse literature and spotty direct interviews. Hence proper state of the art measurements appear on a parameter versus time chart than on a smooth line.

> ➤ A curve representing a stable rate of change is more likely to approximate the true pace of technological progress. New technologies will tend to advance faster than those which are not so new, and individual component parts of total technology will advance at different rates. Hence potential advances in a total operating system should be checked against the progress of its various elements. Any rational analysis must therefore establish not only where a technology lies on its particular learning curve, but also what particular predictive function most appropriately describes its probable unique future progress.

> ➤ A very far of prediction is often harmful. Projections beyond the normal development cycle for the technology increasingly run the risk that basic science or entirely new approaches will completely revise the field.

There are two very big parts that can be put in comparison in the research vs development. Here one is research intensive and the other is development intensive.

R-intensive:

> They work with indefinite design specification where the duty of the R-intensive is to evaluate and implement different alternative solutions rather than think of a single solution.

> They tend to broadcast objectives and market data among technical people, rather than channel specific kinds of information to individuals. They use broadcast communications and few other communication tools to stimulate generation of alternatives that will be consistent with top management objectives and strategies. With multiple objectives it is easier to redesign the work structure and use different tools for measurement of the different other communication tools like journals, internet design, E-commerce.

> They are non-directive to work assignments. It is very important to note that R-intensive programs create the task force but they do not involve people too much. It is self assertion that creates much of the work.

> They maintain a continuing project evaluation and selection process. In this factor a move by a competitor, or results achieved on another project, may obsolete a piece of research or change its priority. This calls for revision of projects to bring in changes.

> They stress the perception of significant results. Group integrated projects have time taken success. But self asserted projects need a mentor and self-understanding to reach over there.

➢ They value innovation over efficiency. Economy in performing research is less important than achieving a markedly better solution with clear market or profit advantages.

D-intensive:

➢ Well defined design specifications. The technical task in this is not to create new alternatives but to reduce available alternatives to a single solution for implementation.

➢ It consists of highly directive supervision where the work to be done is highly interrelated from the beginning of design to successful testing; managers tend to specify objectives, give orders and carefully measure performance.

➢ Another important part is the sequential arrangement of tasks where unlike the R-intensive task where many people can work in parallel on the whole problem or on different aspects of the same problem, the D-intensive organization requires a disciplined sequencing of tasks, with sophisticated controls to ensure that technical objectives are achieved within planned times and cost limits.

➢ The D-intensive organization is vulnerable to disruption by change, and is severely affected by managerial or administrative changes ordered in specification or objectives in midstream.

In the low coupling specification the R&D, manufacturing and marketing are related by process flow and a single way information flow, whereas the moderate coupling has a two way information flow. High coupling has a two way information flow as well as the R&D and marketing are interrelated. All these lead to the customers direction. Downstream coupling brings a success in the company's production process.

In the case of product life cycle, life cycles may vary in length from few months to years. In the short cycle the theory of competitive intelligence is very much required, an alert company should plan to be among the first to bring out a new product to break into a new market, since competition thereafter will generally force prices down fast, depressing profit margins and return on investment.

High investment ratios have four significant implications on management:

> ➤ This requires a wide variety of technology procurement alternatives: whether to buy technology through licensing. Whether to buy a company in order to acquire the latest technology, whether to hire top people or develop internal competencies.

> ➤ High investment ratios accelerate product and process change. It depends on the investments made in one factor and the subsequent one that decides the rate of growth of product and process and the investment requirements needed to understand the changes in both and the environment and competitors involved to understand the nature of growth in that.

> ➤ They usually mean a dynamic product market. Product market should be composed of multiple products and similar competition but usually this competition is targeted by international firms that create the major threat. They create products that can target innumerable markets.

> ➤ They require closer supervision of technical efforts because their market is too vast for only a particular set of skills and they require people with multiple skill assets to win. This requires supervision and teaching for long period of time.

The rigid prescription of a planners mind is very necessary to be understood:

> ➢ Written prescriptions do not always have an impact on the planners mind, and they don't score much of an impact on operations. Whereas other management groups scored stunning strategic successes with practically no output at all of formal statements.

> ➢ Predictive economic concepts on people aspects is very important to be managed.

The inside out approach rests on four assumptions:

> ➢ In an affluent highly competitive economy, success in corporate life as in individual life, goes more and more to the company performing a task with superior ability.

> ➢ A company can create a market by what it does at least, if it does the job well. It is for this reason that the inside-out philosophy may lead to different objectives from the outside-in approach: under the latter approach, the forecaster cannot anticipate what new buyer desires may be created by a talented company's actions.

> ➢ No matter how much market creating ability a company has, it cannot go too far to create new markets. Sometimes extensive market creating objectives are rejected for marketing reasons.

Delphi method is a very important factor of using it in an industrial environment. It moreover starts with perception of need for and feasibility of new product or service which leads to appropriate modifications of long –range R&D planning which leads to evaluation and revision of corporate plans and objectives.

In present times to work on the competence it is very important to work on the venture concept of innovation. There are many tools involved in ventures that helps a firm grow, gain competitive advantage and provides the right direction for its employees:

> ➢ A venture is more unidirectional. It is chartered for a single purpose. It always knows what business it is in.

> ➢ A venture is multidisciplinary and consists of the skills of marketing sciences and product research and development and finance.

> ➢ A venture is entrepreneurial. Market opportunity and cost accounting are combined together. It is also a fertile training ground for future top management.

> ➢ A venture is judicious bringing together alleged markets and product concepts with the concept of selling the right products in the markets with legitimate patent rights and tariff rights.

> ➢ A venture is kinetic standing ready to fill new needs and explore into new businesses.

A venture manager in order to gain competitive advantage has to possess various qualities that would later bring him into the top level hierarchy of any other manufacturing firm. It consists of technical resource or materials or processing expertise consisting of a supplementary resource of knowledge of a specific material or processing technique. Another of venture managers qualities are market resource (market need seeking research and market segmentation expertise). A market resource has two aspects (market research and knowledge of channel and distribution in specific markets). A financial resource consists of cost/price analysis expertise

The selection stage consists of external market opportunities and internal technical and marketing capabilities. It is then transferred to phase B which consists of market need and corporate capability appreciation, with financial feasibility research being the core concept. This leads to product concept formulation and testing being the core concept which leads to market acceptance analysis. After this comes the go decision which ultimately leads to preliminary market potential plan which leads to market entry plan. A preliminary long-range market potential plan, outlining recycling types of alteration in marketing strategy which may be required to ensure achievement of the products planned ROI over the course of its life cycle beyond initial market entry. Recycle strategies are market resegmentation, changes in advertising theme, packaging adjustments, product variations, and price inducements.

It has been seen through years of expertise that it is very necessary to integrate acquisitions. The author of "The acquisition process" Robert A Howell proposes a system whereby management can place the entire acquisition process in perspective, plan growth strategy in a manner consistent with corporate objectives and insure certain integration and organization of companies. The acquisition process is very important to notify:

> ➤ If the primary focus is based on gaining financial benefits and making financial structure much tougher then the strategy formulation consist of rapid growth by acquisition, highly diversified program, and emphasis on financial relationships. The type of acquisition under this is financial- with neither the market served nor acquisition of products by acquired company relate to those of the parent company. The second phase is the investigators and selections which consists of search and management evaluation before the acquisition is done that can change the

global perspective. A quick evaluation has to be made that would make it clear as to whether marketing, manufacturing, product descriptions and what would be the (needs, wants, demands, supply) qualities and how the firm should reach out to move ahead. If finance seems to be the key area of understanding then objective seems to be getting maximum point of view within limits of corporate financial resources.

> If you look at all three perspectives then there is always a slow growth by acquisition but if someone looks at only two perspectives financial and marketing then there is moderate growth. The growth rate often depends on the nature of the company being acquired whether it has a double digit growth or whether the company s production is too outdated or product configuration and development phase is difficult to change. In the case of applied marketing the products manufactured does not relate to that of the acquired company. It is mainly manufacturing that sometimes becomes so similar that if everything is similar then, product life cycle decreases, industry life cycle becomes stagnant and the brand image of the firm goes down until the divesture of a personal unit or a new acquisition is made. So it is very important to focus only on one unit or a particular channel.

After an important acquisition is made future demand has to be forecasted to live up with the change and to see that innovation and all other factors that drives change forward can make the firm move ahead and prosper. A marketing research manager spends two or three days a month reviewing the economic indicators that might aid him in projecting cyclical turning points, predicting economic climate likely to prevail during the forecasting period and yield a forecast of industry sales.

To look forward to understanding the competitive situation a firm has to:

➤ Apart from the Porters 5 forces the firm has to look at other key factors like number of competitors, kind or nature of the competitor, trends i.e. where they do business, how they set up strategic locations and how they understand their resources. Resources consist of various organizational skills, technology creation and adoption, communications as well as different economic predictions. These are the 5 basic strategies before making an uncertainty analysis and using the Porters 5 forces.

➤ This in turn is related to company strategy which consists of task of company manufacturing function and company manufacturing policies. These two factors should never get limited or draw backward as they have a high impact on economies of scale and technology. Any change in competitor or leader processes should not hinder their growth. Market study and the ability to draw a link between the production processes and international patent rights is very important.

➤ There is a long chain from raw material source, to manufacturer, to wholesaler distribution, to consumer purchase, to consumer user to post purchase service. The economic strength consists of analyzing the economies of scale- which is affected by totally integrated production, ability to finance large-scale R&D effort, long margins and relatively fixed cost of sales coverage. The marketing strength may consist of key technical or developmental skills, significant product advantages, exceptional service capability. This is a key process of showing the power of a company and in many cases the company's economic power got limited and showed vulnerability. But putting more dependence in the relationship between raw material source and manufacturer is very important. Economic vulnerability generally has a serious effect on technology and other technology related factors thus making the marketing and channel sales very vulnerable.

Thus after making an analysis of all these factors it is very important to take a drastic step in not only research but other common factors like marketing and technology. It is very necessary to use forecasting skills in all these cases and it is very necessary to properly design the long range planning in case of product designing and resource allocation, because they both are key factors in developing the future of a company and protect the firm from any economic instability.

Chapter 3

Future challenges of marketing in product innovation

By: Baisham Chatterjee (student UNBSJ)

To start this chapter it is very necessary to say that the product managers role is very important in planning for and managing his assigned product line, after which other factors like marketing come into play. Product manager analyses the market conditions and requirements and made sure that his product programs were implemented. He could authorize departures from the approved pricing structure, change priorities on development programs, and approve and implement promotions. His other function is to see that the duties beyond his responsibility is properly carried out. There are certain steps that can be taken to overcome the product pitfalls:

➢ Clearly establish the need for product management.

➢ Ensure proper attention to organization fundamentals.

➢ Develop a manning speculation that is realistically required to handle the assignment and provide for their thorough training. Most technical companies should feature more on the HR training and development, which is very critical for companies with changing technology.

Very often the product manager receives orders. This is very often adjoined to buyers costs which talks of:

> ➢ The total cost of placing the individual orders throughout the year. The larger the order smaller the expense.

> ➢ The cost of maintaining in inventory the goods ordered, while they are being used or consumed, it is very important to maintain the balance for understanding buyers and suppliers needs.

To bring stabilization of different kinds that would help support the goals from a marketing & product manager would be getting at one symptom of business cycles, namely, fluctuations in the rates at which individuals, industry and government spend money. Fluctuations in spending reflect directly on production scheduling. Expansion or curtailment of automated manufacturing is so costly that its advantages are quickly lost when production fluctuates. A research program is very important in order to make the forecasting correct. Judgment and research going together gives far better results. Early determination of whether the product-promotional combination clicks with consumers, using of concurrent testing where possible, examining interim findings- all have been suggested as ways of speeding the research process. Clearly defined priorities, on-going assessments and deletion rules save both time and money. In the mechanics of organizations the committees and factors that help in creating a major impact in businesses are: consumer research, shareholder research, consumer-interest committees, marketing codes, consumer & government liaisons and consumer relations. It is very important to understand the product development process which consists of the following steps: product ideas and basic strategy, feasibility and concept testing, product development and consumer-use tests, marketing plans development, test marketing and evaluation and finally going or moving towards the national program. In order to manage a product important considerations of the product life cycle are: products have a limited life and often features are added to it to change the model .As in modern different features of cameras and stereos. Moreover product profits tend to follow a predictable course through the life cycle. Products require a different marketing as well as production and financial program in each stage. Based on all these viewpoints and past analysis of leaders and originators of the products, imitators can manage the product life cycle. It is very important to create a product review system that would automatically assess the marketing, manufacturing, purchasing, control, accounting & finance and R&D in a company. It is said if the product scheduling and its implications are managed in the creation and operation of the annual product review system then everything is possible very quickly.

The first step that comes first is the creation stage. It consists of:

➢ Appointing a product review team that would hold meetings to set objectives and procedures related to product pruning. It is very important to analyze the product differentiation to address a segmented market, because it is to be noted that a Microsoft Windows software or a Dell computer do not need a segmented market but products from software firms like Oracle or from Xerox do need it. Hence it is very important to plan and prune the product.

➢ After this step comes the operational step: 1) In this the controllers office fills out product data sheets which is then transferred to different software that assesses and restructures the product through specifications of the product manager according to the needs and requirements of the product . Thus giving it a symbol of performance and brand loyalty.

2) But sometimes the necessity to drop or keep a product moving comes from analysis and

planning on the benefits that the product can create and the duration for which the product can benefit. Many computer simulated equipments, defense equipment and drugs have various lethal side effects and destructive power. So even if a product may be very creative it can be dropped. Competitive advantage arises not in the nature of product you create but how you can address and promote the product.

There seems to be always a challenge behind obtaining collaboration and coordination in managing research, sales and production specialists. The best way for that is to use teams or committees in which the members have learned to fight constructively with each other. Effective coordination seems to result when they are in a sufficient low level in the company structure to have detailed technical and/or market knowledge bearing on the conflicts they try to resolve. There seems always to be a required collaboration which can be achieved by:

➢ The sales department in dealing with the market environment to extract information about market trends and customer needs.

➢ The R&D can provide data about any new technical and scientific feasibility of any new product development.

➢ The production department can give a very good feedback on the plant processes and the limits of resources from the production capacity and the need for better production methods. It is the production department that can combine with the sales and research to improve the methods of improving capacity and bring into view the theory of mass production.

There are three different processes known as market environment, plant environment and scientific environment. The market environment consists of (high change, low certainty of information, immediate needs). Plant environment consists of (low change, high certainty of information and immediate needs). Scientific environment consists of (high change, low certainty of information, low range needs:

> The market involvement consists of sales involvement creating motivation to sell new products, mutual confidence in sales market appraisal & research's knowledge of science. All these bring out two things customer needs and new products.

> In the plant limitations production involvement creating motivation to change processes and bring a mutual confidence in the production's ability to produce and research's ability to develop processes.

> Computer simulated projects and business software are creating a wide impact today. Research helps in creating this knowledge and this MIS and E-business helps in gaining further technical feasibility and develop with time.

There are different specializations created between department and the environment that has been talked about. Competitive advantage arises from having a clear understanding and certainty of what the organizational structure should be now? And how it should change in the future. Departments with frequent performance and innumerous levels of hierarchy are highly structured and provide very specific individual and departmental performance. Departments with rules and regulations and lesser spans of control are bound to succeed. It is also very important to assess the members orientation towards time. Members of a unit have problems of either long, short or middle-range character. It is also very necessary to discriminate whether the members orientation towards others are permissive or directive.

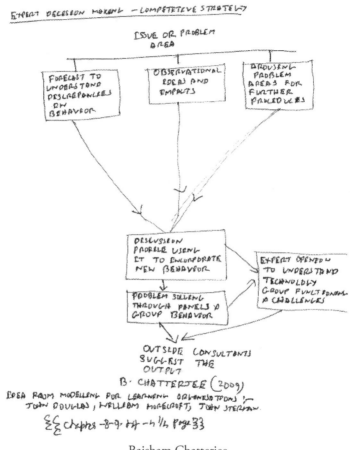

Baisham Chatterjee

In the implications for strategy sometimes or very often raising prices can raise the sales of the product but product uniqueness, brand identity, and understanding customer reactions can definitely help. Moreover factors can be desensitized in two classes- consumer behavior and point of sale variation in marketing impact-produce price insensitivity.

The sale will not be lost until the price is increased more than the value of the desensitized differentials. Due to unfavorable differentials no amount of price increase can make the sale any more lost than it already is.

It should be noted that marketing research cost, engineering development, manufacturing planning, tooling and ingoing manufacturing and learning costs would be recognized as program investment costs. So would be initial advertising, promotion and sales training costs. However, sustaining advertising and other promotion activities would be considered as organization costs.

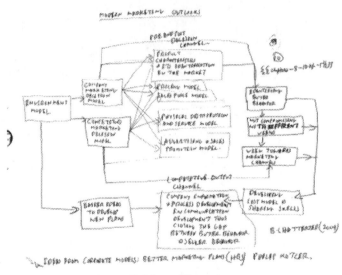

Baisham Chatterjee

Few other factors that should be noted are instances during product maturity:

At maturity the sales volume may stabilize for a long period or may go up or down, since many factors may affect the trend (e.g, new promotional methods, major product improvements, further widening of market uses for the

27

product and product variations.). The maturity zone usually calls for further decisions involving new major expenditures of effort.

To meet all this points you need to take typical marketing decisions:

> Marketing decisions may be like describing market segments with a risk that actual customers not properly identified by a given segment with a possible loss from lost advertising and sales effort.

> Another important factor is estimating future sales and both risks and losses imply that sales may be forecasted as too high or too low. Similarly investment in plants, advertising and salaries may be similar. Future sales forecasting can only be given advantage if the sales is done through benchmarking (a position to improve on).

> Another important marketing decision is adopting straight commission system of sales compensation, with a risk of possibility of high turnover by sales personnel and a possible loss of wasted sales training; customer ill will. It provides an advantage in firms that are generally sales driven (like machine tools).

> The fourth most important marketing decision is reducing prices for the product line, where risk is uncertainty over whether demand is elastic or inelastic, whereas a possible loss is in lost sales revenue if demand is inelastic. The product line defines that products should be mass produced at reduced work load that would automatically reduce the price.

> The fifth most important marketing decision is granting credit terms to increase sales, where the risk stands in whether customers multiply or increase in a difficult to control situation where the possible loss would be customer ill will and inability to collect

efforts. Too many customers make it very difficult to collect feedback and process them to bring about the product managers idea.

➢ The risk can be handled in various ways. The possible risk types are transfer risk to others, handle risk through consolidation, assuming calculated severe risk. There are 4 parts of handling risk through consolidation commercial insurance, self-insurance, merger, diversification which makes us understand if risk is still too high.

Very often there needs to be planning in the supply and distribution of a company and the market segments. In the first step the various decision making and analytic end use of S&D information leads to the second step:

➢ Develop criteria for defining market segments-understand the geographic boundary for understanding the nature of penetration required. The proximity to competitive supply sources should be verified several times. There should be feasible modes of transportation and transportation costs. The price of the products as well as the distance and relatedness between different markets should also be measured.

➢ This leads to dividing the entire market into market segments of meaningful sizes according to the criteria selected.

➢ The previous idea is connected to establish measures of the selected criteria sufficient to distinguish each market segment from others for each means of transportation with an upper limit, lower limit and weighted average (calculated by these methods).All these leads to the third step which consists of defining relationships, market segments, products and supply source. This helps in assessing the market segments and volume of demand of each product. After this comes the fourth step.

➢ The different criteria's of product category or sources of supply are related to determine capacities, bottleneck operations and inventory storage. These three being the most critical and competitive areas. Production rates is another key area of focus.

There are 4 steps in developing a database with S&D model:

➢ The first step is identifying the most important end use S&D information and determining who needs it, for what purposes and how often. The end uses being planning, controlling, contract negotiations or policy evaluation. It is policy evaluation that determines the materials resource planning and everything to outbound logistics.

➢ The appropriate step in classifying market segments, products and sources of supply. An important field of study occupying all these areas are: distance in cluster from ones own to competitors plant, where it would be difficult to make any sharing of critical and important solutions.

➢ The third step is defining relationships among market segments and products. Certain products even with manufacturing interdependence arising from common production processes or strategic needs may have a market in some country and not in other. The cultural association and country needs and wants differences assesses all this.

➢ It is important to determine raw material, production, and transportation cost, and calculating gross profits associated with all feasible transportation modes and routes for various products from plant to market.

The six steps of success regarding the customer service advantage gaining are:

> ➤ Define the elements of service and then determine the customers viewpoint.

> ➤ Design a competitive service package where everything can be assessed through maps and competitor analysis in figures.

All these points are few of the key strategies for market development and areas to focus on. No companies can go without depending on these strong middle level situations.

CHAPTER 4

INVOLVING COMPETITION IN STRATEGIC PLANNING FOR CHALLENGING BUSINESS AND ECONOMY COMPARISON

By: Baisham Chatterjee (student UNBSJ)

There is always a long tradition of portfolio investments in countries. But they too are willing to scrutinize existing and foreign firms. Managerial expectations have changed with time. The 21st century has seen real growth of the product as well as the service industry, with the product market suddenly seeming to be booming. When there is too much growth in an economy government changes the rules and increasingly intervenes. At this point of time of high growth there comes a depression with the equities severely depressed with no hedge against inflation. There is concentration on critical factors like cash and exchange risk. Manufacturing technology is a key determinant of both organizational structure and planning systems. International integration in low density companies is at the functional level and manufacturing technology largely determines the relative importance of such area and functional integration. Automobile production lies somewhat in the middle of cross border operations and mobilizing its resources in national boundaries. Product design and manufacture tends to focus on a geographic region like Western Europe but with limited amount of product flow between regions. Competition may be fierce in the sales and product assembly and relocating, time management in other countries. But this can be well managed through the growing need of virtual communications and networking which makes things easier and enhances performances. Automobile firms have always succeeded becoming big or earning a brand equity because of so many magazines and journals as well as its representation in the world market and strategy for years. Sometimes it seems awkward that there seems to be no competition with all automobile firms tending to grow bigger. But it can be best assessed from the Porters five forces of a cars other components like tyres, hydraulics etc.

In any big firm the marketing and sales team take up sales demand forecasts for the next 5 years. These initial forecasts are passed on the production and buying functions, who build up cost estimates and identify any fault in capacity constraints. Demand, price and cost estimates are then combined to produce profit projections, together with estimates of capital needs for any new capacity, working capital requirements and cash flow projections. In addition to these numerical forecasts the product managers also list their own objectives for their specific product, highlighting strengths, weaknesses, risks and opportunities and their short term tactics. A computer model that makes sensitivity to changes in environmental variables by means of numerical forecasts is used in testing raw material price changes, competitive actions and the like. Gaps in performance opportunities bring new product opportunities, although product introduction planning does not itself form part of the annual planning cycle. Ideas like Porters scenario planning provide greater scope for imagination and flair in pursuing major discontinuities which help in illuminating relevant uncertainties, scan likely futures and be internally consistent. Thus a scenario planning helps in building on all the gaps talked about. A future scenario has strong features like strong political leadership, strong links with international trade system and be more concerned with the trade growth and looks at the governments processes and policies that foster it. A scenario as well defined in the book competitive advantage helps in conflict between forces promoting and opposing growth, government intervention in the market economy and lower growth of international trade. Moreover it is also very important to understand the market quality and industry feedback position which seem to have become a significant part of E-commerce.

In the case of any business it is very important to invest and grow. Growth strategies are very important, mainly for the intensive pursuit of market share, earnings generation subordinate to building dominant position, focus predominantly on long term results and payout and emphasis on technical innovation and market development. Moreover the idea of growth evaluation, capital spending and project authorization is very important. It is very true that integration between product, geography and functional activities is very difficult, but phasing of investment projects is very difficult. Licensing seems to be another important area of being successful in a very competitive environment:

> There should be choice of reliable, competent and compatible licensee with inherent value of the patents, trademark or knowhow licensed, through advance research and understanding of the market.

> The licensor should have a margin of technical and research lead, provision and sales assistance. There should be correct timing and pacing of licensing activity. It is also very important to measure contract obligations and relationships.

There are certain political risks involved as a firm grows bigger, which are as:

> The basis on which funds may be remitted. It is also very important to set transfer prices as well as build a social and economic overhead. It is very important to take access of host country capital market and price controls applicable to sales in the host country market.

➤ It is also very important to look at the limitations on securing raw materials and components, limitations on nationality of personnel. There are often various disputes arising in cross –border planning. The HR has to use their competency to understand and regulate leadership as necessary and help in the dependency of the firm on its internal factors and build on buyer and supplier bargaining power and threats.

➤ It is also very necessary to understand degree of co-operations and negotiations and understand in which countries they can invest, so that they don't have to divest their business or make a loss at certain of their units as Standard Chartered Bank faced in South Africa. Or neglecting to certain extent countries like Ghana, Indonesia and Mexico.

Sometimes to reach standards of global marketing, it is very necessary to reduce the autonomy allowed to local subsidiaries. Industrial products tend to have more standardized approach and greater involvement, while consumer products are more variable, although where standard brand names are used decision-making is usually more centralized. Companies with high levels of autonomy tend to be those that market products subject to local adaptation or who have expanded overseas by process of acquisitions. There are few things that corporate marketing decision makers have to keep in mind before target marketing like: data collection, maintenance and dissemination, quality improvement in marketing decision making, marketing idea dissemination. The international product managers do not alone have the power to decide what product should be manufactured where and where it should be introduced. But moreover a product managers will and ability is determined by a knowledge of the product's profitability by geographic area and the position it has reached in its life-cycle in each of the markets, the collection and dissemination of local market data and the approaches the product has made because of its multiple features to penetrate in other areas. Sometimes the product managers look at product functional aspects like local ergonomics requirements, special needs for size dimension standards, attitudinal constraints and available supportive services. It is also very important to look at the competitive viewpoint like unique selling points of competitive products and product life-cycle expectations. As a reason of greater standardization decision making autonomy has been reduced locally. Changing rules in ideas of selling through distribution channels could convert an operating decision into a strategic issue. The control over creative content is usually highly centralized for basic themes and the use of brand names and trademarks.

Firms should carry a long run self interest and a strong public image. It is very important to carry parts of corporate social responsibility. Firms should avoid government regulation and have social-cultural norms. To hold a strong balance of corporate social responsibility it is very important to maintain stockholder interest and employee morale. There are always three schemas for identifying social responsibility. The first thing to start with is that: there should be an appeal for legitimacy; by confining legitimacy to legal and economic criteria only. It is very important to consider broader extra-legal, extra-market-criteria for measuring corporate performance and social role. If someone looks at the social obligation perspective exploitative and defensive adaptation of costs, there is maximum externalization. Response to social pressures and activities pertaining to government action are other measures that can be used by means of effective PR or a threatening market position that can be acted on legally based on government position.

There are many effective means of competition that are looked upon to be important in an open economy as most of the developed nations seem to be. It is very important to determine production capacity, short run price or output and other non-price dimensions of the product such as quality and variety offered and persuading other market participants. The strategic choices of the competing firms are reconciled in the market by rivalrous processes that consist of the key market parameters.

As talked about previously as in the case of multinationals as also the economy: it is so that if the sellers can segregate the home market from the domestic market the concept of dumping comes into action. Other things equal, discriminating monopoly is more profitable then single monopoly. The industry's average cost may diminish over a substantial range of outputs so that so that scale economies are important relative to size of national market. Export opportunities increase even without price discrimination because an expansion of output is associated with a reduction of average costs. In an industry sheltered from trade the profit maximizing scales of some enterprises may be smaller then the scale that minimizes unit costs of production. Under the assumption that transportation and distribution costs are on the average significantly less in national markets, than for goods shipped between them, with specialized variety of goods with higher demand being produced in larger markets and being sold in smaller markets. A monopolized export industry may practice price discrimination against the domestic market and thereby export more than a competitive industry would.

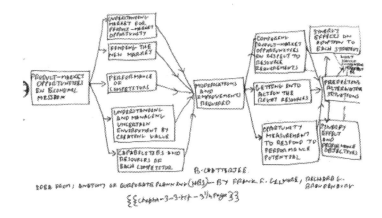

Baisham Chatterjee

Market power in the retail stage is also an important area of study. The concept of concentration differs from retailers and manufacturers however. Concentration of sales of a given manufacturing industry's output in the largest retail firms is one important dimension. A product is modified by the presence of alternative retail channels for the product. As the retail market is generally local, the concentration of a products retailers in relevant retail market is important. The breadth of a retailers product line protects against a manufacturers threat to withhold a product. As discussed about in the earlier product development stage, it all depends on consumers process of choice. The retailers influence in the purchase decision increases with:

> ➢ The benefits of the range of information disseminated by the retailer relative to the availability and cost of information from other sources.

> ➢ The larger the investment information the consumer chooses to make more would be the capacity of analysis and protection from both sides. But the investment should not be too much for a single consumer. Rather too many consumers can distribute it between them, collaborating together.

Unlike an emerging economy as in a purely competitive economy no firm has the incentive to advertise since products are undifferentiated and competitors numerous. In countries where significant products and firms occupy significant shares of the market, however even the firm with an undifferentiated product can benefit from advertising. Previous research in industrial organization has treated advertising in isolation, it is clearly linked to other aspects of industry structure and firm behavior, including some that go well beyond market power. There is a very important source known as Consumer Reports that provides information about differing sets of product attributes and involves differing acquisition costs to the buyer in time and utility. As products vary in costs and other utility-affecting attributes, the optimal investment in information designed to increase utility by selecting the best brand changes in general. The prices of messages sent by information sources, including the advertising media are central data in the firms optimization process. A main factor and situation of advertising is the competitiveness of the media that supplies those services to those markets. This competitiveness is enhanced by the largely fixed nature of production costs of print and broadcast media, which creates strong measures to cut prices to fill advertising space. Rivalry among firms affects the profit-maximizing levels of advertising and other forms of sales promotion. Competitive behavior and inducing too much of competitive movements or recognition of mutual dependence may limit the extent to which sellers bid up advertising outlays competitively. Recognition of mutual dependence may shift rivalry from price to nonprice forms such as advertising.

Retailer power provides a motivation for advertising. If the advertising increases entry barriers, the advertising may be increased beyond the point at which its influence on demand equals it cost. Similar to advertising R&D too has certain components. It involves technical opportunities to innovate. High rates of new product innovation should be associated with high rates of advertising, since introduction to new products imply buyer demand as previously gathered information about market alternatives is made obsolete.

R&D as a percentage of sales is a measure of the inputs to innovation. A firms optimal level of spending on R&D depends broadly on four factors: a prior probability that expenditures on R&D will yield innovations in products and processes, the resources available to innovate mainly knowledge and training skills, the competitive incentives to innovate, the cost of any alternative means of gaining access to innovations besides doing R&D. R&D spending and R&D expenditures they go together and come across and are successful with something known as technological opportunity. Technology opportunity comes from the embedded technology within the firm, the innovation opportunities present around the world even if they are not applicable to small economy's setting. Though the resources rationally invested in innovation clearly depend on the profitability as well as financial sales. There are many things that come into play like working capital, operating capital or help from outside profits. The third factor influencing R&D capacity and spending is the incentive to innovate. It depends on the reduction of the firms performance due to lack of innovation. One benefit is that the firm can stop imitation by other firms. Thus patent rights can save this but what matters more is the differentiality of the product. Differentiality provides the firm with the incentive to innovate to enhance differentiation of the product. It prevents firms from competitive corrosion arising from innovations from others. The basic strategy is not to consider the sources of entry barriers directly but rather to employ the proposition that the industry's level of concentration in the long run will make clear about the entry potentiality with lower concentration showing easier entry.

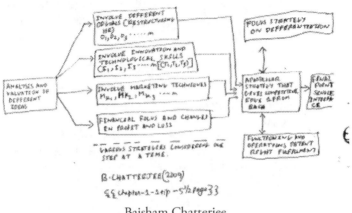

Baisham Chatterjee

Moreover looking closer to the multinational firm perspective as talked in details before: foreign ownership seems to have a negative impact in non-convenience goods because foreign direct investment multiplies the number of domestically produced products and fragments the market. Foreign owned firms bring cost advantages in the form of reduced product development and marketing costs, enhancing this effect.

The different analysis made amount to much less than a full model of determinants of a firms growth rate. There may be substantial differences among large companies in firm specific assets that are intangible or hard to measure-technological knowledge, marketing skills, heterogeneous natural resources, pure managerial and organizational effectiveness. The coefficient of industry growth in concentrated industries is surprisingly insignificant though always positive, and its coefficients exceeds its standard error. For companies in the less concentrated industries there is no relation between company and industry growth. The superiority of related diversification cannot be demonstrated from a cross section of firms unless the differences in the base industries is controlled to depart the sampled companies on their routes to diversification. There are few ideas on increasing assets through competitive diversification which are as:

- ➢ Single product firms enjoy market environments relatively secure from domestic and international competition, although they also lack resources for diversification.

- ➢ Dominant product firms have diversified only slightly because their base industry demands large scale and capital intensive production.

- ➢ Assets and qualities like skills and technology help in entering diversified activity, with the present skills being the core competitive advantage for further improvement.

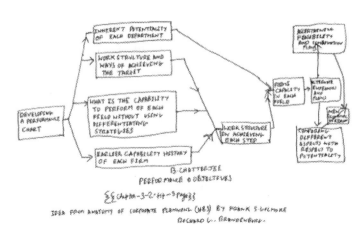

Baisham Chatterjee

Thus losing ones investments because of unpredictable demands or cost shocks is greater if the investment is made in the competitive firm rather than in monopoly (case of monopolistic economy). Power, size and demand insulates a firm to some extent and protects it from cost shocks or different changes in monetary policies and financial debacles. The profit-maximizing firm combines factors of production in such a way that the ratio of the marginal productivity of one factor to that of another varies inversely with the ratio of the marginal factor costs. Thus in industries where fixed assets are relatively important in the production process and are quite durable, long term funding is more efficient. Few other ideas of policy are as:

➢ High concentration does reduce allocative efficiency in some industries despite the openness of Canadian economy.

➢ The present levels of concentration are necessary for efficient scale production in some Canadian industries but probably not all.

Thus competition seems to be a very important force to concentrate on for driving open economies like in North America where the economic environment leads to building a strong demand of all of its products and innovation can be drive by concentrating on the product and market characteristics.

Chapter 5

Achieving synergy and competitive advantage in large businesses

By: Baisham Chatterjee (student UNBSJ)

There are many large businesses that find it very difficult to adopt to very strong and positive economic situations that have originated from a negative cycle, but sometimes the strategist has to take a view at all the possible situations and strategies before heading forward. Whatever maybe the nature of the business maybe it is present in Canada or in Europe, there are many firms that manufacture more than two products or has more than two businesses. This is when a proper analysis of communications in interrelationships come into play. The most important way in achieving synergy is resource sharing or understanding how the positive points or benefit of one can help the other. It is both in terms of economies of scale and used technology, SCM, channels (how far the global network has taken them) and product competencies. It is very important to recognize the costs and benefits of specific circumstances. Knowing when to perform interdependencies may be crucial as knowing when to seek them. Using horizontal strategy to exploit this opportunity would be a critical way of making this interrelationship successful.

Synergy can be viewed as one of the major components of the firm's product-market strategy. It is concerned with the desired characteristics of fit between the firm and its new product-market entries. There are 4 types of synergy based on components of ROI:

- Sales synergy: Using common sales administration, distribution or reputation.

- Operating synergy: Results from higher utilization of facilities and personnel, spreading of overhead, advantage of common learning curves or common inputs.

- Investment synergy: joint use of plant, carryover in research and development, common machinery, tooling.

- Management strategy: utilizing and sharing managerial ability mainly creating a team to identify problems and solving them.

Diversified firms are of 4 types: horizontal, vertical and portfolio.

Vertical organizations have high degree of centralization whereas portfolio organizations have low. The size of central staff is large in case of vertical organizations, whereas the type of decision making is hierarchical in case of vertical organizations, lateral in case of horizontal organizations and autonomous in case of portfolio organization. On suggestions of nature of control vertical organizations have vertical integrations, horizontal organizations have horizontal coordination and portfolio organizations are self administered. Vertical organizations have a high total firm perspective.

There are various kinds of interrelationships that can be found in diversified firms. The various types of interrelationships on which everything is differentiated are: linkages in resource sharing, number of resources shared, number of activities involved and focus of economies.

Most of the firms in the US have diversified businesses because presently the US and the even the EU are getting huge prospects from investments in emerging nations.

Businesses with attractive structures prevent excess resource sharing and does not compromise future profits. In big companies with global presence skills and resources-operate in a globally integrated manner for particular areas of expertise like Warner-Lambert.

Sharing activities can provide a number of operating benefits. Sharing should be on basis of:

> ➢ It takes place between activities that are a significant portion of total operating costs or assets. It reduces the costs of performing shared activities which may be achieved through improved capacity utilization.

> ➢ Sharing firstly helps in understanding ones competence and places where they can improve. A manager or an expert can analyze the consequences of sharing. Sharing helps in product differentiation and helps the firm move down the learning curve faster.

> ➢ Sometimes resource sharing could have a negative impact by reducing the flexibility needed to compete in an environment that demands creativity and quick changes. In research firms sharing is more probable at the lower level than at the top level of hierarchy.

In order to keep moving any firm has to create new value to defend market position. To reach this position, any firm has to focus on few factors which are as: market interaction or being accustomed to the market situations, changes, turnover and customer profile and making a valuation of all this together. The next major point is competitor interaction where the different competitors have to be assessed, for same products or firms which are looking for similar growth potentiality, growth markets or compete to fill the same market gap. Competitive intelligence and idea of future resource idea and procurement helps in this. The third major point is environment interaction where the firm has to look at carbon emission, building hybrid vehicles and respond to climate changes and other conferences to stay afloat in competition. Building on sustainability from environmental issues is a key issue to deal with today. The fourth point is resource deployment where both internal resources already made in use or in process as well as resources that are available outside and are to be brought in future. Oil and gas companies are built with such an infrastructure. All these together combine to form planned activities where the firm takes advantage of future prospects and how it is possible to manage all this in the long term. Another very important factor to address in the planning of activities are day to day cost advantages which can be challenged by competitive offers but are driven by improved logistics, better technical advice or levels of customer service which can provide a monetary advantage over their competitors.

In any firm that needs to grow and prosper needs to have a market control dimension by creating entry barriers, control over suppliers, control over customer access to competitors. Substantial economies of scale deter new entrants by forcing them either to enter an industry at a large scale-a costly action that can give a serious reaction to existing firms- which would suffer substantial cost disadvantages associated with small scale operation. Patients, proprietary technology and established brand loyalty can also make it more difficult for prospective competitors to enter the industry. It is very necessary to restrict buyer access by putting more emphasis on open innovation, global popularization of the brand and making it more popular through communications and internet this would to some extent stop buyers from reaching at other innovative products from startups. But for new companies there are long term success challenges and create an open niche not yet filled which would further have a serious impact on competition. It is generally seen that firms which target a niche market have superior quality of their products. This is the first situation of a firm tending to grow bigger and bigger firms have to relocate and use various infrastructure and technology communications prospects to overcome the threat of a new entrant that relies on E-commerce and channels to make their products popular.

It is very important to access the impact of new technology. With an integrated marketing and communications it is possible to identify differences among competitors, price decision making can be affected if the technology as in biometrics is completely new and is able to provide an enhanced value and altogether different output. Suppliers can have the right idea of competition as they would sell parts to many not one. Hence lesser suppliers can also create an impact in the Porters five forces by increasing the number of buyers and leaves an impact on the financial structure and marketing and sales in the value chain. With the prospect of popularity of a new technology it is very important to cut production costs but few other factors may be more beneficial. It may increase the overall production costs, raise the break-even value or increase the customer lead time. Few very important points that can be given a major focus are: giving power to the people and encourage the culture. Only if a large organization gives power to its employees to authorize certain situations which only he can manage otherwise it would have been difficult. It is also very important to give opportunity to the country where the organization is investing in or give benefits to the channel who are exporting the products to a certain country.

Large organizations has always got to think of competitive strategy from which all other developments come into play. Things like managing environmental uncertainty through the uncertainty analysis, analyzing the industry maturity, capital intensity, size of the organization, external controls of the organization and various aspects of organization structure. Study of the organization structure is very important and gets more complex as the firm grows bigger. To start with competitive strategy after going through the generic terms, and differentiation focus it is very important to focus on the strategic plan intensity. 1) strategic plan intensity and performance will not be strongly associated with one another in firms with low cost strategies. 2) strategic plan intensity will be strongly and positively associated with performance in firms with differentiation strategy. 3) the relationship between use of strategic plan intensity and performance will be positive in emphasizing competitive strategy segmentation.

There are various competitive methods that consist of(durability in the strategy and assumptions that should be assessed to be correct to support the generic strategy), this leads to generic strategy(giving the overall direction of where the strategy would lead to i.e there should be a single goal for a particular strategy but there may be multiple strategies in HR, marketing, technology development and different sub parts of the value chain required to reach there). This leads to competitive positional advantage or assessing generic strategy with supporting competitive advantage). They all together lead to firm performance which is the main goal. Sometimes there are many stuck-in –the-middle strategies, at this point of time it is very important for a firm to look at cost, differentiation, focus as their major advantage which would further help in innovation and increase patents. Innovation helps new businesses to develop their own strategy which the leader can learn from (starting from scratch). Such a strategy of knowing the bottom line and specific niche zones is very important for the leader so that they don't get stuck in the middle and they stay afloat. Clusters as in Silicon Valley and Hollywood play a predominant role in that.

It is very important to find the relationship between different clusters. Finding a relationship helps rebuild strategies. It is true that sometimes relationships are broken due to a certain failure of the product or inability to grow by appreciating a different culture, or being unable to verify the flaws and weaknesses. This is when with the W being very difficult and the T or threats growing. This is when clusters play a vital role with both the leader and the follower learning from each other through interrelationships. This brings no threats and minimal weaknesses, which would be difficult to be controlled until any economic downturn.

Organizational success is a very important factor which is possible by searching for competence. There are three groups of competences: the content of the actual strategies; strategic change competences and strategic learning competences. Closest to the heart the outcomes that impinge on the dynamic marketplace are known as core content competences. Processes like architecture building including prospect of development of infrastructure and communications and calculate it on a time basis in very important. Other distinct advantages are distinct product/service advantage and cost management which are very important after a certain duration when the industry is at its middle stage of growth. The competences are compiled by an outcome of effective strategic leadership. Where the main idea is in reflecting on the ability to add value, ability to innovate and networking for synergy. Which all arise after the first instance of generic competences is managed. Attractive products and services, linked to appropriate customer-interaction processes satisfy customer expectations. Particularly successful organizations will allow the organization to stand apart from its competitors in some valuable and distinctive way. Organizational processes keep cost at a level below the income received from customers. It is very true that in order to reach at fulfillment level the firm has to concentrate on the generic competences. These competences consist of awareness and learning competences, content competences and process-change-competences. To reach over there the firm has to look at ethics and social responsibility, failure and crisis avoidance, strategic avoidance and control, quality and customer care, strategy implementation and stakeholder satisfaction. To start a business in a different situation it is ethics that helps in curing any impediments that the business may face. It is not only talent but very often ethics that helps in crisis avoidance.

It is quality that helps in understanding the CRM impact that the firm may face.

There are strategic architecture competences that makes the organization behave in a coordinated, synergy-creating manner, integrating functions and businesses. The architecture helps in organizing the value added network that links the manufacturer to the retailer and intermediaries, to be managed as an effective integrated system. The systematic thinking leads to synergy from the fostering of interdependence between people, functions and divisions in organization.

It is performing in clusters that help in performing better by understanding ones generic competences. Individual skills and activities - clustering and interacting with one another. In this phase the agents, technology dependants, different component makers and high technology manufacturers try to lead effective control of manufacturers. There is always a tendency to induce strong budgetary control in understanding and bringing a strong reform in analyzing the position of the firm and the restructuring capacity.

There is always a gap between resources, competences and competitive advantage. It is the resources like environmental as well as human, financial that lead to understanding the competences, that would help in further developing the growth process of the firm. There is always a thought process gap involved in that which can be understood and come closer to without having a knowledge gap and technical expertise. The level of bringing these ideas to a success and using ones set of expertise can reduce flaws and put the firm forward by giving them competitive advantage. It is the dynamic process of marketing that helps reach near to that with a result oriented value. It is very necessary to understand the 5Ps of marketing and believe in creating a strong marketing foothold to reach over there. It is very important to find flaws whether the firm may be customer driven or idea driven. In reducing the gap the time frame should be managed in reaching the spot.

Computer generated information system, spare parts centre, training programs and advisory functions are other means of resources for understanding and reaching near to understanding the core competence. After that everything is a thought follow-up. Marketing seems to be the grand competence in understanding product value-generating exchange. A strong marketing controlled company has a lower turnover of dealer and more concentration on personal sales and networking. It is long-term relationships that help in understanding the transformation skills and the grand competence of marketing. Thus it is the transformation skills in marketing that helps in determining how far a firm should imply its skills and how it can apply its competence to bring its synergy.

CHAPTER 6

STRATEGIC ASSUMPTIONS ON INNOVATION BY DEVELOPING ON COMPETITIVE STRATEGY

By: Baisham Chatterjee (student UNBSJ)

It is economics that determines the micro-production units over time as computer technology and administrative practice have improved. Statistical agencies have focused on producing a set of industry statistics at a point of time. Many examples can be give from several studies correlating economics to innovation using financial strategies and advanced technology.

1) It is the market structure that first comes into play. The most commonly used measure of structure-concentration-depicts the firm-size distribution at a point of time. The dynamics of changes in firm size have long been suggested, but require the researcher to follow plants and firms over time. Few measures show substantial stability, the industrial system has come to be characterized in many circles as being relatively rigid, and adaptation as difficult and slow. Firm size distribution is an important area of study for developing economies and is an important idea of concentration statistics.

2) Merger studies have considerable pressure for more information on effect of mergers. Merger waves gain public attention and spectacular failures lead to legislation that affects the market for corporate control.

3) Here in general the ideas behind different theories in industrial organization has been discussed. In this case because of the large number of changes in the corporate form of the organization, production entities can appear to be new when all that has really transpired is a change in corporate control.

It is to be determined that the number of firms entering and the number of firms leaving cannot be determined that easily because they leave at a ad hoc basis. Different countries have different ways of managing new enterprises as well as firms going through long periods of losses. Firms may go out of competition in few hours in case of small businesses that may be highly virtual or technical due to big flaw or technology lag. Similarly firms that drive with entrepreneurial spirits may end their run due to financial debacles or misfit in communication. The unmanageable gap creates most of the problems. Moreover inter firm cost differences create other market entry differences as well as makes competitors difficult to understand the strategy of entry of its various units. Thus it is difficult to control or manage the strategies of growing businesses or businesses with several units targeting different market gaps.

International competition is another key area to concentrate on with allocative efficiency and productive efficiency being the major areas of study. There are two assumptions that can be made relating to international competition. They are as:

1) Transaction across national borders that encounter large natural (transport, marketing) and/or artificial (tariffs, quotas) restrictions that do not impede domestic transactions.
2) A heterogeneous buyers taste of differentiated goods that might be nationally distinctive; and the costs involved in differentiating the product.

It is also very necessary to understand the productive efficiency have emerged from employing different production functions to estimate the gaps between average and best-practice plant productivity in individual national manufacturing industries. In every country efficiency increases with international competition, measured either directly through the imports share of the domestic market or inversely by the amount of protection provided by the government. Moreover international competition improves the cost and efficiency levels of individual firms.

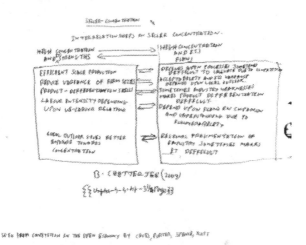

Baisham Chatterjee

Both 1) and 2) have practical approach to world markets and the challenge national industries face:

1) One implication of the smallness of an open economy is that the number of domestic sellers and buyers regularly in the market is absolutely small. Disturbances originating with individual domestic parties then might be averaged out less fully than disturbances to comparable individual parties located

abroad. Trade exposure could reduce turbulence among domestic suppliers.

2) The foreign market being larger, the producer faces a more elastic demand in the international market. Trade exposure increases the relative the relative sizes of quantity responses to disturbances from either foreign or domestic sources.

There are various ways of measuring turbulence which can be defined by understanding and verifying the different competitive forces like entry or when a new plant is created in an industry. Other factors regarding to the most evolving factors of management are exit, gain loss or merger. Merger is defined to occur when the ownership of plants changes.

To determine the different innovative aspects involving the different management perspectives the aspects to be looked upon are success within a particular industry, size class, or technological emphasis. It is very necessary to have success in small firms in the industry growth stage; competitive pricing is associated with small-firm success in the mature industry stage; and aggressive marketing strategies at the time of decline. Technological improvements in communications and transportation, coupled with globalization of markets, have brought out the theory of tackling the factors of intense competition. To look at efficiency improvement the firm has to at least use new materials, use existing materials more efficiently, reduce labor or energy costs and look at just in time inventory control. Process improvement helps in rapid product evolution and controlling the different areas of business and different segments of the business arena. there are different weights for comprehensive marketing which come as a very important criteria for further developing new products: maintaining current products in current markets, introducing current products in new markets, price relative to competitors, quality relative to competitors, customer service relative to competitors and flexibility in responding to customer needs. In the comprehensive labor skills required it consists of innovative compensation packages, importance of other staff motivation strategies. During the product life cycle more emphasis should be given on production efficiency which helps in realizing market share gains. Comprehensive innovators make way of innovative sources of financing and it is less risky than the product innovation stage. The firms involved with management innovation place a higher value on innovative organizational structures, management incentives, compensation packages and adherence to total quality management.

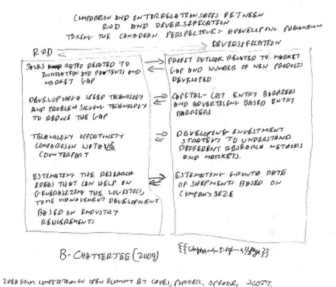

Baisham Chatterjee

Corporate diversification is another area to deal with to understand the modern economy. Firms with multi-unit operating structures spanning different markets play a significant role in economic sectors. It bears issues on competitive strategy, industry growth, resource efficiency, economic power and market structure. To present diversification statistics for all major economic sectors based on employment characteristics of multi –unit firms. It includes diversified firms with production units in different industries and consolidated firms with all units in a single industry. Also the geographic characteristics of different firms have to be investigated. We can examine corporate diversification into broad and narrow spectrum entropy in respect to horizontal and vertical diversification in respect to inter-industry commodity flows. Concentration, growth, average firm size and knowledge intensity have also been put into use to understand the diversification within an industry. Expansion of the firms operating structure helps in giving importance to inter-industry commodity flows in order to separate industries in related and unrelated groups. Broad spectrum outlook helps in mitigating demand shocks whereas having a narrow spectrum outlook helps in creating more of a demand shock. Diversification occurs more in industries with higher concentration, higher profits, lower growth and lower exports but these effects are only evident when through the multivariate analysis variables are affected with one another. The industry diversification in this case is quite specialized. Diversification can help in acquiring operating units in different industrial sectors. The several factors used on this are-the need to capitalize on vertical efficiencies by establishing control over discrete elements of production and distribution chain, the desire to take charge of special assets like R&D and the idea of reducing exposure to demand shocks by spreading risk over different product markets.

Computers are transforming the technology set and changing the way in which manufacturing establishments do business-by changing the way products are designed and engineered, the cutting and shaping of parts, the assembly process, the planning and control of material requirements and integration of these various processes. Computer-controlled equipments measures the output and ascertains reliability before producing goods. The input into the computer led manufacturing process- materials planning- combines both product and service and the service costs often far outweigh the cost of manufactured product. Changes in relative labor productivity, employment share, and relative wage rates demonstrate the effect of advanced manufacturing technologies on the input mix. All of these may be due to a variety of reasons like demand for skilled labor, increases in productivity, or an increase in the complexity of products or its processes.

To improve the performance measurement plants may either improve their relative cost structure or may be able to produce high quality products for which consumers are willing to pay higher prices. In either case what is expected is higher levels of labor productivity relative to industry mean, where the growth in market share is accompanied by relative labor productivity. The grouping is done on behalf of measuring the performance- market share growth, labor productivity growth and profitability growth of a firm relative to other firms in the industry. The more successful firms tended to place greater emphasis on R&D capability and R&D spending which help in developing new technology. Difference in the emphasis were accompanied by differences in R&D activities. Moreover more successful firms use R&D tax credits. Sometimes it is important to know whether external, long term debt financing limits the ability of the firm to invest in soft knowledge assets like R&D. it is important to note as to what improves our understanding and drives the relationship between R&D and capital structure. R&D collaboration and partnerships is very important, they are performed extensively in partnerships, alliances and joint ventures. This collaboration helps in reducing risk and speeding up the product cycle and reducing the cost. Collaboration may be across borders as in the case of large organizations or between a large organization and a creative local firm to sell in the home market. Collaboration is mainly made to make the technology and R&D processes much better. Firm ownership and its hierarchy and the competitive environment helps in giving opportunity to the firm for further development and progress. Foreign subsidiaries perform R&D in Canada more often than domestically owned firms. A breakdown by sector of activity shows, however that technological opportunities and imperatives existing in research intensive industries force the majority of firms both domestic and foreign in the core sector to perform R&D. Foreign affiliates are also more likely to complement their own research and development activity by participating in joint ventures and R&D partnerships.

To put innovative ideas into practice, firms rely on a combination of internal and external sources for technological competence. Canadian firms have difficulty in using internal resources available within a multinational network and generate their own technological expertise through research and experimental developments. Another particularity of foreign owned firms is that they rely more on technology of unrelated firms. Even though collaboration with universities and government is more advantageous for domestic firms but the brand name of a multinational creates core prospects for doing research in Canada. HR too plays a key role in innovation with majority of the compensation packages being given to innovators in the service sector.

Linkages are a different form of connectivity between the industry and the customers as in forward linkage or between industry and suppliers backward linkage. Certain forms are relevant to the Canadian business after years of research on Michael Porters linkages. Inter-industry purchases or sales comes in terms of backward or forward. Firms in this dimension may be into similar business or in differentiated or dissimilar businesses. Linkage is divided into these two groups because it is thought that the incentive to create innovation networks would be quite different for firms within the same industry as opposed to firms that are connected by goods flows across industries. Supply innovation linkages are seen to involve substantial interfirm co-ordination, in that they involve finding new ways to use materials. A costly process rebuilds old processes of developing a product in different ways and thus requires the reengineering of a firms production processes. Firms face impediments to devise these types of innovation partnerships with supplier firms, its severity is in the costs of developing partnerships. It consists of fixed cost-that is, a cost component that is not related to the size of the goods flows between two industries. Linkages control an important factor in production economics. Moreover marketing is a very important area of success and bringing new products which is a key area of difference between an innovative and non-innovative firm. The differentiation between more innovative and less innovative firms are in the form of: There are various R&D capability and research agenda; accessing new markets, especially export markets; the frequency with which new products are introduced; using the different criterias of technology like borrowed technology, own technology, patenting and securing new technology for future use etc. Other forms are controlling production costs by using new materials, reducing energy costs, and using existing materials more efficiently; making use of government programs for export assistance.

There is no correlation between output growth and initial labor productivity growth. That is if population of plants are divided into two groups based on initial labor productivity at the beginning of the period, we cannot predict future growth in market share or in labor productivity. There is a strong correlation between output growth and labor productivity growth which can be defined in two ways. First labor productivity growth may improve efficiency, allow a plant to reduce its relative price and allow it to increase its market share. Secondly increasing market share may increase profitability and lead to more investment thereby increasing labor productivity.

Labor productivity growth is negatively correlated with employment growth. Those plants that expand market share also increase employment, but there must be enough other plants also increasing employment - those losing market share - that the overall relationship between employment share and labor productivity is negative.

Among the innovation regimes the main characteristics lies in competitive environment, strategic orientation and innovation which are represented at a broad basis by:

➤ Communications is a process by which production technologies are changed and low liquidation value for machinery and equipment are key sources of uncertainty. Strategic orientation may be to use high quality suppliers and purchasing technology. In its innovation characteristics innovation seems to be a legislation obstacle, which can be tackled by confirming product quality improvement and reliability and acquisition of major channels.

➤ In the financial services category consumer substitutability and threat of entry are dominate sources of uncertainty. Excluding product development customization strategies are a more intense area of competition. Intense price competition is also an area of competitive environment. Incentive compensation plan and training and development are more intense strategic skills. In the innovation characteristics reducing unit labor costs is a relatively more important objective. Competitor analysis and use of trademarks and certifications is very important.

➤ In the technical business services in a competitive environment there are many important secondary sources of market uncertainty with product obsolescence and difficulty in predicting competitors actions. To look at the technical perspective refining technology is a very important aspect. In its innovative characteristics customer diversification and product flexibility is very important whereas speed of delivery and user friendliness and adaptability is very important. Another important characteristic is a more diverse use of intellectual property rights. But there are often financial restrictions and labor shortages.

In order to understand and minimize the gap created and bring a turnaround in networking and information transfer firms should develop cost advantages and depend on the generic factors before moving to the Porters five forces where the other factors may be determined. But as a firm grows bigger starting from a small business, cost differential and external contacts play the most important force in competition. Collaborative research is another form of research which is better than joint research which otherwise becomes difficult to overcome certain problems. Thus cost advantage seems to provide key product advantage that drives product innovation.

CHAPTER 7

VALUE IMPLEMENTATION BY MEASURING THE VALUE CHAIN

By: Baisham Chatterjee (student UNBSJ)

Value is determined by the utility combined of benefits delivered to the customer less the total costs of acquiring the delivered benefits. Value is then preferred combination of benefits compared with acquisition costs. Relative value is the perceived satisfaction obtained from alternative value offers. A value proposition helps delivering value to customers. A value chain is a business system that creates end-user satisfaction and realizes objectives of other stakeholders and enterprise functions that occur in the maximization of value creation. The value chain understands and modifies the mission of an organization, hence the value chain becomes a design for the business mission. Customer value is composed of customer value criteria and customer acquisition costs. Value proposition is a key success factor that brings value strategy and positioning that maximizes the efficiency of different factors of the supply chain including production and different cost drivers, which ultimately combines together to improve the organizational structure.

There are many important individualistic phenomenon involved like value/cost drivers like time to market. Other important factors pertaining to the logistics is rapid response/delivery that is important to a customer at low/optimal costs. After-sales service may be more effectively delivered by centralized specialists. A strong marketing and distribution company has all these characteristics. Value chain components consists of the most important customer value criteria like security, performance, aesthetics, convenience, economies of scale and reputation. It is combined by customer acquisition skills which consists of installation, maintenance, disposal and various service skills. This together leads to adding customer value like results produced for the customer and process quality and price to the customer and cost of acquiring the product service. Profitability and productivity are key success factors required to manage information and finally manage the coordination and coproduction in relationship management. Organizational structure management and operations structure management consisting of sourcing and procurement are the key factors involved in delivering value like time to market, service, quality.

In any measurement graph it can be found that process technology consisting of manufacturing and logistics, customer segments and customer applications consisting of product technology help in developing opportunities and structures to help in managing a highly skilled business through a very segmented and coordinated outlook, so that the business does not get disrupted.

Cost minimization is an important criteria of the value chain which helps in gaining cost advantage. Hence to participate in either product /service differentiation cost efficiencies has major attraction. There is always the impact of new technology in operations management which is a derivation from the financial structure and strategic investment management. Flexible manufacturing systems, just-in –time helps in further development of new processes and helps in differentiation at an accepted cost level. Thus this helps in developing core competencies that outsource those activities that may be performed more cost-effectively. This helps in core business activity and understanding how to manage fragmented markets. Supply chain automation and electronic communication are other important forms of reinforcement for making processes in the value chain much faster. While bringing this into action few things have to be kept in mind like customization design, competitive pricing, performance and features, economical operation, capacity and productivity arising from R&D advantages. Very often technological factors are involved in relationships like technological linkages involving: design, manufacture and sales. Advanced designs, time to market, tested ideas are important ideas behind the value creators.

In the core processes involved in value chain it is completely linked to managing the supply chain after managing the demand chain. Few qualities of the supply chain are : efficiency focus, processes focused on execution, focusing on cost by making it a key driver. Short term oriented decisions regarding the demands which can bring an impact on the immediate and controllable future. Things involved in this are tactical manufacturing and logistics personnel. Other important factors are immediate resources and different constraints that help in putting an impact on the value chain. Other demand chain analysis factors are putting into action a product market fit, processes and revenue. Other factors are long term oriented involving planning cycles that help in developing different planning schemes that involve the technology development with different support services. There are also different means of analyzing macro-market characteristics which consists of analyzing business environment and identifying product-market gaps. It is very necessary to understand market segments and understand market segment volumes. It is necessary to identify price points and ascertain different purchasing and consumption influences. It is very necessary to ascertain acquisition costs and identify the required assets.

Another very important point of analysis is the value chain methodology, where the different components of the value chain analyses the business potentiality. It is very important to determine a target map which will carefully identify the structure of the business. It is very important to develop whole chain current state map and develop issues and opportunities to develop future ideas and recommendations for modifying the value chain. In understanding the customer analysis it is very important to understand the visibility of actual weekly consumer demand all along chain and get a single forecast for the whole fundamental chain analysis. A coordinated management policy and forward prediction of what would happen in the next 5 years and then making an overview of what would happen later makes an analysis of the requirements and necessities for the future orientation. Stock reduction and quality management helps in creating more consistent measurement and feedback.

It is very important to understand the partnership sourcing which calls for joint strategic planning and problem solving: information sharing; synchronized accounting, measurement and reward systems, sales staff motivation and rewards. It is also very important to build momentum and search for progress. In bringing out different criteria of understanding the boundary mapping of the value chain. Each firm develops its strategies and plans independently of the others which involves sales targets, production plans and others. There are various possibilities and potentialities of the value chain like accounting measurement and reward system measurement. Sales staff they give their targets. It is very important to understand the legal and regulatory tradition and competitive confusion. Other factors involved are lack of trust, and slowness in new managerial skills. It is very important that the value chain is reconstructed properly so that the value chain can ascertain the future impact of business. There are many different internal processes of the value chain but the main factors that can be associated with that are supplier value, channel value chains and buyers value chains. It is very necessary that very often and moreover always costs drive the value. It is very important to understand the buyers value chain and make a state of sustainability of the value chain. The value chain can last longer through proper coordination and maintenance of the company's processes and understand the various aspects of the cooperative intensity of the value chain. There are potentially unique competition factors that are within the firms capability to bring about. To cooperate in these factors the different focus factors are leadership, workforce caliber and corporate renewal. There are many distinct competency maps involved including routine competences.

There is a very important research framework that is very important. This research framework consists of information distribution, information synthesis, information organization and information gathering. These are the factors that carry forward in understanding the support activities that are involved in understanding the creativity and different innovativeness of the organization.

Any process, product, person or brand that adds value to a product or service constitutes a value chain. People who add value are generally internal consultants, creditors and shareholders, marketers and channel partners. Typical ideas are product and process based technological evolutions, insourcing and outsourcing. In case of changing international trade policies and market forces that constitute the major part of the product. It is very important to mark the main idea development behind product criteria and its specifications. As stated earlier it is often the product manager who handles these duties. Other factors involved are communications architecture and inbound and outbound logistics that control these products and the factors that generate knowledge. Sometimes value chains become complicated during co-creation and co-ownership of products. Sometimes during an alliance when product research is handled by two firms. There is no clear definition of where and how to capture the market. Very often when products are handled by a firm with more creativity than the other the strength seems to be more distributed and seems that technology development and integration is the leading priority. There needs always to be an ideation to manage this. Managing key suppliers and discovering new dependencies is very important. Through new collaborations it is easier to design and restructure new processes and technology profile. Suppliers seem to perform a key role in the value chain. It is very important to identify the category of the product portfolio and the different types and developments that can be created through this. But very often problems arise from all this. It is very important to identify, analyze and resolve these problems. It can be done through continuous improvements. This study is composed of leader analysis, past history and entrepreneurship and leadership ideas that can help in developing and giving a further improvement to the product and the business. Another important form of collaboration is known as the value net because it creates value for all its participants- company, suppliers and customers- and because these participants operate within a collaborative digitally linked network. Similarly for companies that design their businesses around it, a value net is a practical strategy for providing what so many internet-age consumers and business customers now demand: customized products, fast order fulfillment and products bundled with services they value. It chooses customers carefully and assures of fixed deliveries. It is very important to manage the value chain components as the processes flow carefully. It consists of product-service specification and design, procurement and inventory management, marketing and sales, value delivery and customer service management. This is well managed through a superior CRM and supplier relationship management. This is all related to innovation paradigms and keeping its flow. There can be cooperative innovation both between pharmaceutical industry and Dell computers. The innovation is so well set up that it leads to bringing the different characteristics of the demand chain. There are various factors that regulate the organization of the product-service specification and design and helps in value delivery and distribution. There are various innovative assets that undertake the strength of innovative capabilities. They are as control and coordination criteria, operational gearing criteria and financial gearing criteria. The cash flow which is an ultimate result of the value chain has an impact on the assets whereas the capabilities has an impact on the strategic idea, revenue and operational idea behind the cash flow. Sometimes Porters value chain is extended in upstream and downstream direction, with external networks being the support activity and supply chain management, product use and end of primary use being the primary activity. All these coming in the form of a customer concerned value chain where the main focus is margin and brand equity. Product use comes after marketing & sales which is very integral part of the customer knowhow. The service ends it to bring brand retention and this leads to brand equity. The internal value chain of Walmart suggests that looking for new products and suppliers is an integral primary activity of a retailer. Whereas purchasing and inspection, stocking shelves, and advertising and promotions to get customers into stores are other primary activities. Real estate is a very important support activity that controls all these. Thus for a retailer a value chain will obviously be different from a consumer electronics manufacturer but the later moving in the direction to support the retailer. Other integral parts are aggressive deployment of systems and technologies that help it reduce shrinkage and internal costs. It is very important to control the value chains relationship with suppliers and the enormous economies of scale it achieves through hard bargaining and purchasing in large quantities. Another important aspect is enhancing customer experience in the store. This is how a customer led value chain works.

Cost benchmarking is another important factor that can help companies reduce costs involved in the value chain. It can be identified by comparing key drivers involved in the cost like people, purchasing, R&D, process improvement, salesforce, transport and efficiency in raw materials and time management.

This situation of time management is very necessary to reduce costs and are always involved in big companies which tend to manage a very effective global supply network. This carries the main idea behind technology development and internal policy management and its throughout improvement. Information systems forms a key role in bringing this cost reduction after measuring all the factors involved at present and all the factors that can be added in the future.

CHAPTER 8

GAINING COMPETITIVE ADVANTAGE THROUGH A BREAKTHROUGH IN DECISION MAKING

By: Baisham Chatterjee (student UNBSJ)

It is very important to understand that breakthrough ideas create the major impact in decision making and makes it clearer as to the nature of ideas required to reach the breakthrough process or understand the factors that can suppress it.

There are many contingency factors that can lead to thinking deeply of the nature of breakthrough ideas like:

> ➤ A major technological breakthrough in hybrid cars or biometrics can be foreseen but its timing cannot be determined presently like using a new manufacturing process for that.

> ➤ An economic recession which would lead to loss of order for the particular biometric product and would change the pattern of spending.

> ➤ A major economic depression.

> ➤ A limited war for a limited time period that would increase the demand of other related and combined products.

A few very important diversification objectives to make a follow up of the breakthrough ideas are:

➤ Everyone is well aware of the different diversification methods and a vertical move to contribute to the technological progress of the present product line.

➤ A horizontal move to improve the coverage of the biometric market.

➤ A very important choice of direction is to increase the percentage of commercial sales in the over-all sales program.

➤ Using a lateral move (going beyond the confines of the industry) to stabilize sales in case of recession.

➤ A lateral move to broaden the companies technological base.

➤ It is very important to generate further focus on simulation techniques, feedback control system theory, and analysis of decision processes are being developed in the engineering and research developments of many firms.

Using these breakthrough ideas to bring a profit potentiality, would be like:

➤ Each diversification move is characterized by a transition period during which readjustment of the company structure to new operating conditions take place. The measurement of the profit potential should span a sufficient length of time to allow for effects of transitions.

➤ The firm should search for alternative environments although business performance will differ depending on economic-political environment.

Profit potentiality is a long term factor but to respond to short term changes in the volume of sales they might respond to three basic cost categories: product costs, committed costs and managed costs.

It is very important to create advertisement prospects to increase the profit potentiality. It consists of public, prospective purchasers, inventory information and sales information.

In order to bring a proper function of the HR or the work environment that would lead to gain this advantage are: routine tasks which consist of filtering- separating, assigning priorities to and screening data for routine handling. Load sharing-relieving overloaded situations. Load balancing-taking action to balance the work load of subordinates. Adapting- employing forces appropriately in changing situations. Adjusting- dealing flexibly with new situations or problems. Communicating-receiving and imparting information. Interacting- handling the interrelationships of managers and employees. Coordinating-acting in common with others. Checking- preventing, detecting, and correcting errors. Expediting- speeding up progress and dispatching work promptly.

It is very important to think of PERT thinking it to be a very important tool in electronics industry. It consists of a network to manage events and activities or the major steps in the operations of the business. An event represents a specified program accomplishment at a particular instant in time. An activity represents the time and resources which are necessary to progress from one event to the next. Secondly events and activities must be sequenced on the network under a highly logical set of ground rules which allow the determination of important critical and subcritical paths. Thirdly time estimates are made for each activity of the network on a three-way basis, i.e., optimistic, most likely, pessimistic figures are estimated by the persons most familiar with the activity involved.

The idea of analyzing equipment needs to manage breakthrough ideas is very important:

- ➢ Convert the proposed product plan from dollars to units, by years and by product group.

- ➢ Let the plant manager select for each item the route sheet that represents in his opinion, the average manufacturing time for current products. For future products he can make estimates on basis of time for current products with similar manufacturing process.

- ➢ Multiply the manufacturing hours for each product by the unit-volume forecasts for each year.

- ➢ Cover setup time, sampling error, inefficiencies and sales fluctuations. This gives the total operation for each product.

- ➢ Subtract the total operation hours represented by inventory on hand.

- ➢ Convert the difference into the number of pieces of equipment needed or the bench requirements.

It is very important to note that an organizations objectives are made for the long run. Its long run investments in research, organization, public relations, institutional advertising which may divert profits in the immediate future. It is necessary to understand whether the firm has made a good profit-and-loss showing without cutting back its investments in manpower, supervision and training. Very often to predict a long term future assessment division's ambition conflicts with needs of the corporations as a whole. In such a case it is very important for the division head to work hardest in the way he knows best.

Long range planning is very important to develop competitive strategy structure which can be given a forward development by starting to develop on the platform of the organizational structure. Long term planning may be a difficult job but it is a very down-to-earth assignment which makes a team approach absolutely necessary. A new method of projections has been derived from marketing variable analysis. The really basic problem is to decide what kinds of products, selling, expansion, and organization the firm should have and to keep company activities balance at a period of expansion.

A five year summary plan for a company can be achieved in various ways: with the first year dealing with improvements in customer relations and service which stands as a support factor in the value chain. The next year stands as manufacturing reorganization which is a very important form of restructuring or developing certain different processes to deal with variable environmental outlook. The third year stands with separating the industrial division with the vendors and assigning a very global network to support the subsidiary. The fourth year deals with strengthening and developing the sales organization and building up on the research and development. As with all the factors and efforts combined, it gives a very different outlook in the fifth year with a merger to increase productive capacity which would further make things bit more easier adding to lesser complexities which means growing from within. A very important plan tells management – what it is going to do, how it is going to proceed, when it will take action.

There are often success or failures involved in long-term planning. This is when three important lessons come into play: 1) The work should be directed by someone who is in more or less continuous contact with the different managers concerned so that the results reflect a team approach. 2) A long range plan may be so vital that it might be worth hundreds of thousands of dollars to competitors which is a partial measure of the cost. There are six steps which can identify the criteria and ability and duties of the top management:

> ➢ The planning team has to determine the key influences in the growth of the industry and evaluate the influence of each. Sales potentials are obviously tied to per capita consumptions, and management

can project the market fairly accurately barring any revolutionary changes.

➤ The strengths and weaknesses of the company should be accurately evaluated. A strength should be to locate an unit to a country or area where there is something called future sales or government policy of less competition faced.

To bring breakthrough ideas to a success the firm has to concentrate on few versatile models that has the ability to perform multiple functions:

➤ An inventory model will compute inventory level, number of stockouts or delays, the performance of the logistics and number of orders placed. It can also help understand the lead time and the daily demand for materials.

➤ A transportation model can be used to plan optimum means for serving its widely dispersed terminals. In a oil company as in Calgary probable future costs by use of pipelines, barges, tank cars, and so on are being related to projected changes in volumes and product mix at each terminal.

Baisham Chatterjee

The operational models that are developed through computer experimentation are based on the two following factors.

> ➢ How existing production and distribution facilities can be used in such a way as to yield minimum total cost for given levels of customer service?

> ➢ What configuration of production and distribution facilities in the future will make for minimum cost for given levels of customer service?

> ➢ Another very important factor that can be explored and understood are the effect of uncertainties in future costs that can be explored for purposes of selecting the combination of capacities, uses, costs, and levels of customer service which is most consistent with the over-all objectives of management planning?

The business game in long range planning is another important factor that is used in testing useful strategies in allocation of resources under competitive conditions and are constructed primarily for the focus of improving on executive training:

> ➢ Computers make it possible to reproduce with increasing realism a complex business environment.

> ➢ To calculate rapidly the consequences of decisions when affected by random fluctuations in and changed relationships among inventories, measures of customer service, and supply of working capital.

> ➢ An operation is performed to allocate the company's resources to production, marketing, research and plant investment for the ensuing period. After this the effect of decision of the market is calculated based on the business games and the performance of all the teams and the amount of conversion that has been done by each team to reach a definite situation.

> ➢ The cumulative effect of advertising or its decays or "half life" when terminated and the lags associated with implementing the results of research and development.

If someone comes along with a breakthrough idea of starting a business, he has to hit on with the basic ideas of the growth stage. Very often a company's financial capacities, management skills, market rigidities can limit the rate at which the company realistically grow. This growth rate in turn affects total research program size and the internal balance between short and long term offensive and defensive research. After assessing this situation a very important factor is hit upon: Should the company develop vertically towards its markets or raw material sources or horizontally into new areas at the same level of manufacture or distribution? Should it try emerging markets, BRIC nations or traditional markets depending on nature of segmentation created or nature of the product? Should the company be a broad line operation or should it specialize in limited fields?

Moreover a firm has to look at whether it is growing through acquisition? Internal development? Merger? A combination of these approaches? This research approach carries with it certain important areas of focus:

> ➢ The payback period on the growth investment is likely to be longer than in acquisition strategies.

> ➢ Operating and functional departments must be more technically oriented and highly co-ordinated to appreciate research technology and be ready to exploit research achievements as they become available.

> ➢ Research often requires a greater risk on less certain information than do alternative approaches.

> ➢ More fund analysis should be done on the allocation of funds to the long investment cycles that are characteristic of research.

There may be three types of research plans generated in three ways three to five year plans, five to seven years and five to ten years. Few very important research strategies may be: concentrate its research efforts, remain on the grapevine in touch with scientific community, virtually ignore developing technology.

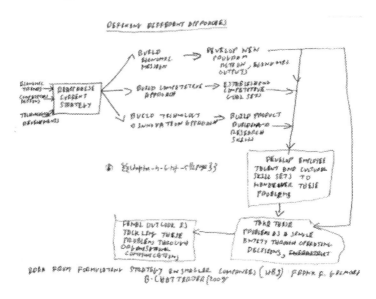

Baisham Chatterjee

The grapevine program is very important in the sense that it should ensure: 1) that sudden advances in certain areas of science will not catch the company unaware and completely demolish a major segment of the business 2) force competitors to cross-license otherwise damaging technology

3) develop market positions for itself and at the same time avoid preemption by competitors.

These are the major skill sets of breakthrough idea that would help in understanding the nature of growth and communications required to provide an advantage in this situation.

CHAPTER 9

TARGETING CUSTOMERS IN EMERGING MARKETS

By: Baisham Chatterjee (student UNBSJ)

Emerging markets are opening up for FDI s. Their industry segments having highest revenue, government support and those that ventured with latest ideas are gaining utmost prominence.

The following ideas for developing business in target segments by satisfying customers' needs are as:

i) Present marketing effort should be taken in relation to long run profit potential of the segments, starting from the time when the smaller companies followed the most dynamic ones till the present scenario or boom when most of these small companies have turned in to mid sized ones.

ii) Marketing models like various means of direct marketing or models of business transaction through retailers or wholesalers have to be developed in order to reach the end customers, to create maximum benefits. These benefits will bring surety and genuineness to their brand image.

iii) For every emerging markets the economic scenario in the country, competition behaviour, national regulations and competence have to be understood to develop a model to target the buyer behaviour. And turn it into maximum satisfaction of the buyer to create dominance of the product.

iv) Customers giving high importance and assurance to the company by buying products for periods exceeding contracts and from whom companies get a huge return should be kept as customers for ever and be given premier identity in the company's interests.

v) The post of "Idea Managers" can be created within a company and such managers should have the clear understanding of multidisciplinary committees starting from finance to major product development. This position may lead to breakthrough thinking and lessen the strategic gap.

vi) Internal employee motivation techniques and developing empowerment and motivation scheme for sales people may bring out a very effective marketing strategy. This would create an effective over all firm strategy. It is important to increase the process of overhauling financial risk and bring about financial self sufficiency. Internal organizational behaviour should also be reformed for a small firm to improve the advertisement and prominence of the product.

vii) A multinational should provide support to all its strategic business units for profit, growth and develop competitive pricing.

viii) Making a prior analysis of marketing channels like internet, mobile capabilities and making a differentiation strategy for various customer segments.

ix) Alliances should also be made with suppliers and strategic business partners, so that networking perspectives for the particular business increases and the owner's interest should also grow increasing the firm's standard.

x) The cost of customer acquisition and cost of customer retention should remain balanced and it should not increase abruptly or nonlinearly.

xi) Companies must attain a rate of return of 12% and companies that have higher levels of customer satisfaction than their competitors generally achieve a higher market share, attain a strategic perception of quality and can demand a premium price on comparable products or services.

xii) Benchmarking internally as well as externally is very important which can be obtained to get the most correct customer feedback through research. It is necessary to improve organizational performance to gain ability to respond to customer's concerns.

xiii) The people's attitude involved in CRM should be sharp enough to generate additional sales from certain existing customers by using processes like:

1) Developing new and changing product concepts by discussing it with other companies through alliances and research.

2) Saving time in new product development by frequently developing machinery, modifying nature of working and labourers' orientation to a different platform and changing product transformation strategies through more effective financial policies and bolstering R&D projects.

3) Targeting customers through sales segmentation and infrastructure management to bring about a different view of the product which can be felt through the changing pattern of technology and communications.

4) Building the financial stability for the company through sales to those who have understood the image and brand meaning and top management reputation of the company.

5) Some important ways of rating emerging markets is developing a single real time view

of each customer and creating an ability to sell when the customer is ready to buy and knowing how to appeal to the customer in the case providing services, benefits and few returns to the customer.

Some other means are:

1) Understanding the economic situation of the countries that have opened up like in Korea, China, India etc and also the attitude of people in the western world not previously knowing much about the Asian markets and their nature of doing business very recently or within a span of 10 years or so. Most of the companies in the western world hitherto conservative are now very eager to get a market share and cross all the major hurdles like:
    i) Understanding the psychology of the people in that particular demography.
    ii) Finding out proprietors, vendors, franchises in that particular country for the product to reach all the specific locations.
    iii) Make a comprehensive analysis on the thoughts, beliefs, lifestyles and desires of people in that country particularly in relation to consumer durables or textile manufacturers. This is why even after finding ample talent in India, the innumerable types of likings and inscrutable thoughts make it very difficult for many mid- sized M N Cs for doing business in India.

2) Other ways of moving into emerging markets are keeping very good relationship with stake holders because they are the people who enlarge a firm's

vision. This helps in getting key customers for most profitable and trust worthy firms.

Vision goals should be such that the customer can satisfy all its wishes and get a value addition for the price he pays by focusing mainly on short- term sales and also focusing on the business that could have been generated.

Every company should be aware of their most attractive customers or else businesses would not survive whatever may be its international market strength.

To develop a CRM strategy any company should first think about their SWOT analysis like:

3) In case of application services or production every company should think of their most profitable customers and strategies investment plans or innovative machinery for production provided for the customer's satisfaction and this analysis would only help in analyzing as to which are the things they want more

    1. The reasons for putting so much trust on them and not on others.
    2. The effectiveness of each department the seller has and how they can be entwined to make it more efficient through bench marking. This mapping would lead to comprehensive victory over its competitors.
    3. Ideas like giving benefit plans to small companies by buying their product (like seller's brand would help the customer build an image overseas by diversifying its business or through more value addition or addition of features to their product).

Similarly big companies can get a special price, quality, performance offer and warranty in one department whereas in another department these offers can be changed through incredible patent rights of the company.

STRATEGIES FOR CREATING CUSTOMER RETENTION AND EXCEEDING CUSTOMER DEMAND IN DIFFERENT INDUSTRY SEGMENTS

PRECISE STRATEGIES FOR GOING AHEAD FOR EXCEEDING CUSTOMER DEMAND AND CUSTOMER RETENTION	CREATING AND EXCEEDING CUSTOMER DEMAND IN DIFFERENT SEGMENTS	DIFFERENT WAYS OF CUSTOMER RETENTION AFTER EXCEEDING DEMAND
STRATEGIC ANALYSIS • Analyzing the B2B and B2C trends through proper channel analysis • Analyzing threat of emerging industries and impact on marketing. • How time management can change way of logistics and operations. • Verifying sales strategies and procedures in a company. • HR should bring cohesion among the departments **COLLABORATION** • Collaborating with efforts and developments with other fields. • Collaborating and alliances with competitors to win in the market. • Collaborating in a one to one basis. • Designing a financial plan for next two years depending on customer response and reliability	**SOFT WARE (I T)** Evaluate immense competition and then target customers by understanding the demand generation and need of B2B markets, channels **FINANCE** Understand the future investment plans of the B2C and B2B customers by segmentation and micro-segmentation and making the lower level management understand the psychographic and demographic models **PRODUCTION** Understand the capabilities of the new B2B,B2C markets and invest by understanding world wide core competence and develop through B2B experience and thinking of relevant ideas for developing the products **CONSTRUCTION** Understanding infrastructure development through broad analysis of previous tastes and customers expectancy, economy and livelihood of upper class, growing companies, communication, advantage in other countries and their art.	• Building trust and values with new customers • Building long time relationship with effective growth plans and effective and relevant schemes . • Making a proper segmentation to understand the opportunities in the market and target new customers. • Understand the demographic needs and share core competence with competitors or businesses which are not completely different. • Small companies should come up with group involvement strategies with customers to learn more.

Baisham Chatterjee

The attitudes and performance of the customers should be noted and its importance can be measured by:

1) Making an evaluation of the satisfaction level of respondent customers.
2) Research identification of the most probable emerging competitors with similar core competence

Hence customers in emerging markets can be targeted by all the factors as stated above and can also be measured by micro-segmenting customer base, knowing value of each individual which can be done through psychographic models, BI Tools, Data mining, Sales plans, market research etc.

Hence countries should be targeted on the basis of current F D I it is receiving from industry segments from other countries by determining the strength of the receiving country in that area. Moreover, growth, prospect and plan of the country should also be analyzed before targeting the customers in that country.

CHAPTER 10

CHANGING TECHNOLOGY PROSPECTS WITH GLOBALIZATION THREAT FROM EMERGING NATIONS

By: Baisham Chatterjee (student UNBSJ)

There would be a massive change in this hypercompetitive market in the years to come and innovators would try to exceed inventory turnover rate and create a systematic, completely differentiated, and most applicable idea and thought process. Early adopters would go according to the most recent global risk assessment and then verify their internal strength before following the core competence of leaders undertaking maximum amount of risk to achieve highest growth rate.

There should be proper networking in the home country as well as with most of the other emerging and poor nations. Politically and socially there should be integration which would increase localization by giving importance to the country's culture and the benefits other countries derive from that country's exports.

In case of emergence of a new market segment certain factors that are to be analyzed after evolution of the market are:

1) In what way technological change has to be planned so that people understand why they should buy the product or why people should start learning about the segment.

2) When a new market evolves the product innovation strategy should be based on buying power of the target segment (depending on focus market advancement,

growth and alliances they have built in the present scenario)

3) After the phase of market evolution at the key responsibility level when new customers have to be sorted out the new business unit should see that there are no errors in policy making like organizational structural decision making. The firm should analyze risk factors like:

- Market risk or uncertainty of economy and such variable factors like dependence on the most advanced technology depending on companies on which the economy depends, leadership style factors, change in innovation stock and progress of the company.

- The company should clearly assess enterprise risks and country risks which are somewhat linked to the hierarchy levels in the economy (conditions or growth prospects of the economy and depends on the economic strength of the country where the business has been ventured).

- If other external risks as well as above risks can be adjusted then performance will not vary. Similarly brand image can be protected by carefully promoting the brand at least to maximize sales in few segments.

- Competitive risks can be minimized by creating an advantage through ways like forecasting the entire supply chain and creating all the stock for emergency purposes in logistics.

- Building a strong network and efficient marketing channel by collaborating with suppliers, industry associations can be made better by first collaborating with the government.

Say after a span of ten years all economies of the most progressive nations will be a totally integrated economy which would minimize chances of duplication, thus saving costs through standardization i.e. due to this global phenomena innovativeness will increase to a very high extent in these multinationals and this will increase the growth and development of economies. This process will proceed to a certain extent until businesses mainly service firms involving a very high extent of thought process become stagnant and businesses which are more prominent like evolving technology oriented or technology which had earlier not received so much prominence as of today and many people have thought how to develop on that but have failed have developed a somewhat similar but differentiated prominence. These emerging factors would create a major impact on the value chain of the major businesses who have ability to take challenge against the upcoming integrated economy system and see to it that the cost factors like labour costs and other economies of scale don't create major impact on the changing nature of business,but rather sourcing can create generalized growth by helping economies mainly emerging markets because emerging economies do not have the industry infrastructure to supply advanced technologies and manufacture high quality products.

Like integration in the economy integration between the various departments by exploiting the linkages is also very important. Self developed equipment, lower salaries of local employees, increasing local sourcing to avoid government import tariffs and lower costs and increasing competitiveness of the subsidiaries by manipulating the cost effectiveness and defensive strategy of each subsidiary. Small firms with more complex businesses can only block path for other firms and it is only possible until the business gets very diversified. Thus it is more difficult to manage diversified businesses which show some similarity with others. But there are innumerable mid sized consulting and analyst firms in the United states which possess this quality of both market evolution and blockage. New technologies create possibilities and uncertainties in the market and brings about a market transition, makes the growth and development stages of the company more difficult as well as shows that companies should first concentrate more on localization. Many US firms are finding it more difficult to grow further but there are many Chinese firms who have started to grow only because of a few strong leadership oriented people in these emerging superpowers as well as the success of their citizens in the West.

There are two types of businesses existing one of them is product centric and the other is customer centric. Ex Sony's walkman is a product centric business whereas companies like Samsung, Akai are customer centric. In this highly competitive market more companies are getting customer centric. To win trust of customers even a strategic alliance should be done with a market leader in case both of the businesses are completely differentiated. Similarly with growing companies and addition to the number of products and services for targeting a single customer companies are trying for a customer friendly relationship with a very friendly website. Customer profitability is a key area that is to be measured. There are definitely variations in cost & revenues across geographies. But cost of manufacturing or costs involved in making the product reach the end customer through channels are definitely incurred in home country whereas revenues are earned from other countries. This scenario will become more prominent in the emerging nations say after a span of 10 years. Hence creating a global product and customer prospect through present data and understanding both the technical and ethical prospect of a new product to be launched in the market will show a strong sense of what the product should be like. Emerging nations are turning into open economies to understand this. Moreover in this era of competitive thinking along with the rise and decline of businesses which is becoming more rapid the other factor considered:

Productivity: The overall productivity worldwide is going to increase at a very fast pace. Hence due to this growing productivity not only would the academic competition increase but new business formation and economic growth would depend on this. Hence Western firms would look for collaborations to expand their business in Asia although they may be having a majority of market share in Japan. Japanese and Chinese firms generally have the production and technical capacity to develop multiple products for a single capacity.

Hence after ten years businesses would not succeed until they come up with something totally different.

In case of say a pharmaceutical firm like Aventis developing penetration and expansion strategies would be like:

- Market entry and patent right process say for a cancer drug and how their competitors like Pfizer has gone through a particular process of marketing the product in a particular country.

- A mapping should be done based on location of business, environment which would bring out the idea as to which is the best area for investing in a manufacturing plant.

- Global advantage of the product and also the extent of social benefits should also be noted.

- The competitive threats as well as the sale from a competitor of other medicines in different segments has also to be analyzed. The sum total of the revenue, year on year growth, quarter to quarter growth, sales target achieved through pricing and innovation, new product found and their sales turnover; all these factors analyzes as to who is better and more prospective.

- Firms should look for co-marketing alliances to promote high sales even under an uncertain or declining economy. For this it is very important to get more expertise from outside company who may be retired medical practitioners or people with sound sales knowhow and product knowhow of a recently FDA approved medicine.

Supplier upgradation program and modernization of infrastructure are the compulsory factors for FDI.

After 10 years it would be easier to relocate business to many countries which was earlier much more difficult. Because of the melting boundaries and a similarity of businesses between home country & foreign country revenue of firms who have brought out a universally similar global model are the ones who are bound to succeed.

A pharma major looking for double digit growth should concentrate more on growth of healthcare system to focus more on an organization for selling the bulk drugs so that people slowly gain more trust say on an organization who would be supplying all the necessary amenities to patients. Pharma retailers would take charge of the world pharma market and individual pharmacists and physicians will have lesser prominence except in low cost economic zones. Genomic drugs should carry regulation for trials although they may be possessing the insta-cure quality.

Today brand switching has become an inevitable thing because of too much substitutability. But with the emergence of nanotechnology which could be related to such a diverse set of technology that maybe after the next 10 years substitutability will reduce. Till then say after 30 years nanotechnology & biometrics would bring out products for which mass marketing and production for the open market would be compulsory in order to stay in competition. Future market share can be predicted more efficiently only if competitive forces do not emerge randomly from less developed, moderately developed and few emerging nations. Whatever may be the global scenario there should be strong buyer-supplier relationship which would definitely increase efficiency and minimize delay.

As public and private sector firms are investing in the infrastructure development of developing and emerging nations global transactions would reach its peak after a span of 10 years or slightly more and it would continue to increase with more modern infrastructure development and new technology.

It is very important to analyze the superiority of different regions and from which country a poor country in Latin America or Asia can gain from a country with added value and superiority in certain areas and on which factors these things play.For the south-east Asian countries it would be more applicable for them to tie up with countries like Mexico which have core competence in cement, similarly Brazil plays a similar role in food and an upcoming role in textile. Till today countries in sub-saharan Africa are facing political instability, declining real income hence it would be impossible for these countries to emerge as players. These emerging nations would be developing manufacturing and process control ideas that would help in increasing exports and make imports minimum at least in few very thought provoking segments. In the future it may be necessary to build a strong and improving relationship with strong and distant competitors which would help in broadening the product line and multiplying product uses through new product experience.

Customers would generally be sophisticated equipment manufacturing firms or service firms with continuous change in technology and processes and to adapt to change. The ultimate leader would be the one who upgrades its products features or production capacity and have cost advantage and proper understanding of the scenario that is influencing the major trends in the markets like 1) business cycle influence on external investment possibilities 2) customization possibility of the target market and 3) different major areas of growth & competition which the company may shift to.

These are referred to as strata 1, strata2, and strata3 in order.

Strata 1: The business cycle definitely affects the investment possibilities which in turn affects the purchasing power parity which also affects the target market immensely, generally in the long run.

Strata 2: In the customization possibility,ex- an infrastructure firm would always look at countries with growing market needs and investment possibilities but never in a sub-Saharan African country where only non-profit organizations can take up the challenge. It is impossible for an investment consultant to invest in a oil rich nation until they have the expertise for that. Hence technical expertise, segmentation and investment knowledge should come hand in hand in this rapid change of globalization structure.

Strata 3: Any self sufficient economy can look towards creating a robust banking structure whereas a software firm with the best expertise in the world would provide their customers with financial, risk assessment software as well as analytics. Hypercompetitive sectors need cooperation and overseas acquisitions to increase their growth rate. After assessing the risk in investing in these sectors an economy like China may find a core competence in aerospace to look for higher growth and more respect.

These are an analysis of the key factors that can affect global business and managers can bring out improvements on that.

Chapter 11

Competitive advantage involved in sustainable strategy development

By: Baisham Chatterjee (student UNBSJ)

To lead an environmentally sustainable enterprise it is necessary to practice a few elements in management that are recent theories and are used for developing on the most evolutionary technology and best practices in modern world. The main idea behind that is instant market for a lot of products, globally scalable ideas that can be widely understood and accepted and measured by any industry groups and teams working towards the forecasting and future development perspective. Enterprise development is the key area to think of. Other forms are that businesses are built in environmental principles and water, oil, gas are used as regular processes for the survival of the company. It is true that manufacturing is a key and basic area to start with to bring out a complete restructuring and intensive protection of the world economy and innovation. Sustainable strategy is the key reinforcement to customer rights and CRM. Carbon production improvement is becoming a serious issue to concern upon, and this is what would create a better world and economy to live in. It is very necessary to collect energy hubs which would help in future use and empowerment of energy requirements. It is necessary to make GDP expenditures which small companies can take up as a challenge to learn from the market leaders.

It is very necessary to create environmental health and safety organizations and it is also very necessary to look at process emissions which will undertake the idea of calculating the improvement requirements that would further give the idea of future challenges. Another important idea is the hybrid vehicle incentive program where every idea on innovation can be turned around to give the necessary requirements on how to increase the effectiveness of hybrid vehicles. There is need for energy saving and need for innovation in disposable technologies. Disposable technologies as in medical equipments as in bio-medical engineering helps in building on faster production, better marketing and better use, as well as giving better shape and trust for an action or implications made on somebody. Disposable technologies can thus displace stainless steel and create more of a market share on new technologies and innovations that might be more costly. But the cost can be reduced by proper measurement and control, but it might be only for specific use and more or less impossible to use it for bulk purposes even 50 years from now because the market tends to be more open and grow much bigger, where steel production would carry vast effects and better possibilities not only limiting it to construction but also in tool designing. It is very necessary to consider ecological design principles and not product designs. To listen to this global warming phenomenon government must start with this. But it would be very difficult for the government to stop it and reduce carbon productivity, because stopping it stops economy growth and profitability to some extent, although service industries are creating a major shape in any economy. Customers, people, products, clients makes innovation and leadership develop this based on client needs making it dependant on competitive advantage. It is also very important to develop core strategies to understand the different concepts for improvement. It is very important to serve clients using best people and manage them using people who understand both marketing and are inquisitive to R&D which would help them understand new product needs and manage products better. It is very necessary to use clients and case study methods to better understand the usage of the product.

It is very important to look at higher construction costs, lack of awareness of benefits. It is very important to understand the sharing model and send return on investment and understand the model of global impact. It is also very necessary to concentrate on comprehensive utilities, transportation, sustainable demand and education. Probably education and sustainable demand are interrelated to make it clear that behavioral sciences and engineered solutions can proceed in order to develop the relationship between further education and developing a continuous demand of a product through more effective disposable technology. It is very necessary to look at education task force and company energy task force. There should also be a pre-intervention to reduce energy cost, as well as reduce capital cost. It is also important to decrease in research by 20%. The S-lab or sustainability lab can be another important dimension that big firms like Millipore and other big bio-tech majors can have.

There needs to be collaborative portfolio of energy projects and hotspots of energy use. Electricity compensation to reduce 30% of energy consumption. It is also very necessary to increase education opportunities and resource opportunities. It is also very necessary to build technology groups for better understanding of creativity by using communications. At the end of the day there is no proper communications between two sectors and there is very often a transport and transparency issue. At the end of the day it is very important to know how secured consumers are. Leaders can only drive a strong motivational advantage in this behavior stage. Technologies and individuals they choice on how they value technology by making an interconnectivity. If during the behavioral stage people have passion and are persuasive they can use a merger of technology in managing risk and direct future of our business.

As recorded earlier there are few problems in the US energy sector. Transmission of infrastructure is the biggest problem. Ethanol and corn crop is used to produce ethanol. $500 million has been used in the US industry to create better efficiency to produce bio-fuels. Energy needs are used to generate better efficiency so that total energy supply needs are minimum. Until now and today producers know how cost of pricing has been made more attractive. Fossil fuels are used to reduce carbon input of those fuels. Carbon utility bills and grocery stores are used to understand the need for reinvestment in alternate forms of energy. In reality a comprehensive energy filing is required to renew that for the next 20-30 years. There should be a comprehensive national energy policy with oil, gas, solar, biofuels making the complex decisions and tough choices. Competitive pricing and investing heavily on energy renewal would be the most important thing to look at for the future.

To build a strong carbon future by implementing a sustainable strategy there are many ratios of possibilities not politics of limitations, there are also challenges in technology and public policy involved. It is also very necessary to modernize next generation of nuclear energy although the probe for first generation is also involved. There should be an opportunity where right technology can be developed, and there can be a possibility for decarbonization in an energy efficient world. It is also very important to utilize fossil fuel and carbon footprints. Adaptation helps a lot and thus watching the economy and its different connective systems move helps in the long run. It is difficult to suggest a solution until everything is brought together to derive results.

It is sometimes said that often bad things happen to good technologies. Sometimes cost of renewable energy, price of renewable energy and model of renewable energy has to be calculated. A terrific product doesn't generate efficiency or output immediately. Rather it is said that the output comes mainly from proprietary technology where many issues are not deployable. There are many a times that a high thought-provoking technology leads to disefficiency but the idea can be brought back by not making it more complicated but by leaving the clues for further research and development on that. Another thing thought of is static but high technology setting which can improve over time. Other things required for this are a fleet design program and an intensive marketing program and commitment to it. So a lot of research is on the process which can determine the future of technology. Only after the specific technology is determined its impact can be determined.

Conclusion

This book provides various opportunities regarding the different aspects of modern restructuring and competition. When we talk of restructuring we do not mean only talking of an economy or market but also bringing about a change in the competitive processes. In this book **Reconstructing Competition and its processes** I have reconstructed very vague and difficult ideas to give it a clear picture of where and how a business can move forward. I made use of very abrupt ideas and techniques, through my ideas from different books that I read earlier in my career. Before coming to UNBSJ as a student and throughout my earlier life I had been a voracious reader. Few books by Henry Mintzberg gave me a clear idea of how to use very vague ideas. Using terms as in the RAND Corporation and its earlier research and bringing everything together was my idea. I also made many original contributions in this book in reconstructing or developing on them. My ideas were read on the previous books on competitive strategy that I read by Michael E Porter. My charts and models are a percept from the books written by Kaplan & Norton. This book carries vivid ideas on innovation and its hurdles and its descriptions that can create a change in modern developments. These developments made based on the aspects created in different chapters shows the different perceptions of the value chain, its abilities, the abilities and performance of the firm in different economies as well as product capacities and its improvements have been recognized. The various outlines in this book are generally concentrated on Harvard Business Review articles and generally play a key role in the development of modern processes. Most of the articles are around 30 years old but as they provide a sound structure of theoretical aspects, they cannot change, but yet when put in order they can be modified and help to build a new transformational structure. When all the data is collected from the book and more emphasis is given on that, it provides a very different internal outlook on competition. The MIT videos provide a clear structure of sustainable strategy through new technology. Moreover other important areas of function that can notably change innovation prospects is the product study. None of the ideas in this book are from Michael E. Porter (because more or less everyone has gone through that). Its more of a developed phenomenon which few people have thought before to bring together.

Probably innovation is going to change and all firms have to look forward integrating these competitive processes.

REFERENCES

BOOKS

1) Derek F .Channon, Michael Jalland(1978): Multinational Strategic Planning **American Management Association (AMACOM)** 79-87, 105-127,236-249, 285-290

2) Richard E.Caves, Michael E. Porter, A.Michael Spence with John T.Scott (1980): Competition in the open economy, **Harvard university press.** 12-16, 95, 96, 123-134, 143, 165-175, 271, 278, 287, 297-303, 338-339, 354-355

3) Michael E. Porter, The competitive advantage of nations **Free Press** 77-103

4) W. Chan Kim, and Renee Mauborgne, Blue Ocean Strategy **Harvard Business School Press** .37-124

PAPERS

1) H.Igor Ansoff (1964): Strategies for diversification, **Harvard Business Review.** 3-7

2) Marshall K.Evans (1964): Profit Planning, **Harvard Business Review.** 14-17

3) Jay W.Forrester(1964): Industrial dynamics: a major breakthrough for decision makers, **Harvard Business Review.** 24-25

4) Frank F.Gilmore, Richard Brandenburg (1964), Anatomy of corporate planning, **Harvard Business Review.** 62-68

5) Robert W.Miller (1964), How to plan and control with PERT, **Harvard Business review.** 81

6) Bruce Payne (1964), How to set realistic profit goals, **Harvard Business review**. 96-98

7) Bruce Payne (1964), Steps in Long-Range Planning, **Harvard Business Review**. 106-109

8) William J.Platt and N.Robert Maines(1964), Pretest your long-range plans, **Harvard Business Review**. 114

9) James Brian Quinn (1964), Long-Range Planning of Industrial Research, **Harvard Business Review**. 124-126

10) James Brian Quinn and Robert M.Cavanaugh (1964), Fundamental Research Can be planned, **Harvard Business Review**. 140

11) Ronald J .Ross (1964), For LRP-Rotating Planners and Doers, **Harvard Business Review**. 166,167

12) Seymour Tilles (1964), How to evaluate corporate strategy, **Harvard Business Reviews**. 177-179

13) Patrick H.Irwin and Frank W.Langham, Jr (1967), The change seekers, **Harvard Business Review**. 6

14) John R.Shipman(1967), International Patent Rights, **Harvard Business Review**. 33

15) James Brian Quinn (1967), Technological Forecasting, **Harvard Business Review**. 46, 47

16) H.Igor Ansoff and John M.Stewart (1967), Strategies for a technology-based business, **Harvard Business Review**. 62-67

17) Philip A.Scheuble, Jr (1967), ROI for New-Product Policy, **Harvard Business Review**. 78-81

18) David W.Ewing (1967), Corporate planning at a crossroads, **Harvard Business Review**. 103

19) Charles H.Granger(1967), The hierarchy of objectives, **Harvard Business Review**. 118-122

20) Norman Berg (1967), Strategic planning in conglomerate companies, **Harvard Business Review**. 128-132

21) Donald J.Smalter and Rudy L.Ruggles,Jr(1967), Six business lessons from the pentagon, **Harvard Business review**. 160

22) George A Steiner (1971), Rise of the corporate planner, **Harvard Business review**. 6

23) Harper Q. North and Donald L.Pyke (1971), 'Probes' of the technological future, **Harvard Business Review**. 10

24) Mack Hanan (1971), Corporate growth through venture management, **Harvard Business Review**.25-27, 32-37

25) B.Charles Ames (1971), Marketing planning for industrial products, **Harvard Business Review**.46-50

26) Robert A.Howell (1971), Plan to integrate your acquisitions, **Harvard Business Review**.56-59

27) Laurence D.McGlauchlin (1971), Long range technical planning, **Harvard Business Review**.103

28) Dean S.Ammer (1971), The side effects of planning (thinking ahead), **Harvard Business Review**.112

29) William F.Christopher (1971), Marketing planning that gets things done, **Harvard Business Review**.132-134

30) Robert J.Mockler (1971), Theory and practice of planning (keeping informed), **Harvard Business Review.** 151

31) Richard F.Vancil (1971), The accuracy of long range planning, **Harvard Business Review.** 155, 156

32) Wickham Skinner (1971), Manufacturing-missing link in corporate strategy, **Harvard Business Review.** 160-165

33) Tom M.Hopkinson (1965), New Battleground Consumer Interest, **Harvard Business Review**.162-166

34) Philip Kotler (1965), Phasing out weak products, **Harvard Business Review.** 70-79

35) Jay W.Lorsch and Paul R.Lawrence (1965), Organizing for product innovation, **Harvard Business review.** 91-99

36) Robert Mainer and Charles C.Slater (1965), Markets in Motion, **Harvard Business Review.** 103-109

37) Philip A.Scheuble,Jr (1965), ROI for New-Product Policy, **Harvard Business Review.** 124-127

38) Mark R.Greene(1965), How to rationalize your marketing risks, **Harvard Business Review.** 23-28

39) Ross Pirasteh(1965), Prevent blunders in supply & distribution, **Harvard Business Review.** 62-66

40) Philip Kotler (1965), Corporate models: better marketing plans, **Harvard Business Review.** 94-99

41) Mack Hanan (1965), Corporate growth through internal spin-outs, **Harvard Business Review**.113, 120, 121

42) B.Charles Ames (1965), Marketing planning for industrial products, **Harvard Business Review**. 142-146

43) John Baldwin (1992), The dynamics of firm turnover and the competitive process, **Statistics Canada**. Pg2

44) Aileen J.Thompson (2000), Import competition and market power: Canadian evidence, **Statistics Canada.** Pg 5

45) John R. Baldwin and Richard E.Caves(1997),International Competition and Industrial Performance: Allocative Efficiency, Productive efficiency, and turbulence, **Statistics Canada.** Pg1

46) John R.Baldwin and Joanne Johnson (1997), Differences in Strategies and Performance of different type of innovators, **Statistics Canada**. Pg 18-19

47) John R.baldwin, Desmond Beckstead, Guy Gellatly and Alice Peters (2000), Patterns of corporate diversification in Canada: AnEmpirical analysis, **Statistics Canada.** Pg 19

48) John R.Baldwin, Petr Hanel and David Sabourin (2000), Determinants of Innovative Activity in Canadian Manufacturing Firms: The role of intellectual property rights, **Statistics Canada** .Pg 27

49) John R Baldwin (1997), The importance of research and development for innovation in small and large Canadian manufacturing firms, **Statistics Canada.** Pg21

50) John R. Baldwin, Brent Diverty and David Sabourin (1995), Technology Use and Industrial Transformation: Empirical Perspectives, **Statistics Canada**. Pg 28-29

51) John R. Baldwin and Mohammed Rafiquzzaman (1998), The Determinants of the Adoption lag for Advanced Manufacturing Technologies, **Statistics Canada**.Pg 14

52) John R.Baldwin, Guy Gellatly and Valerie Gaudreault (2002) Financing Innovation in new small firms: New evidence from Canada, **Statistics Canada**.Pg 1, 31

53) John R.Baldwin and Petr Hanel (2000), Multinationals and the Canadian Innovation Process, **Statistics Canada.** Pg 45

54) John R.Baldwin and Alice Peters (2001), Innovation and connectivity: The nature of market linkages and innovation networks in Canadian Manufacturing Industries, **Statistics Canada.**Pg 6-7

55) John R.Baldwin (1995), Innovation: The Key to success in Small firms**, Statistics Canada**. Pg 23

56) John R.Baldwin and Wulong Gu (2003), Plant turnover and productivity growth in Canadian manufacturing, **Statistics Canada.**Pg 18-19

57) Guy Gellatly and Valerie Peters (1999), Understanding the innovation process: Innovation in dynamic service industries, **Statistics Canada.** Pg 9

58) W. Chan Kim, and Renee Mauborgne, Blue Ocean Strategy **Harvard Business School Press**

59) Michael E. Porter, Competitive Strategy **Free Press**

60) John S. McCallum, Preparing for an uncertain economy **Ivey Business Journal**

61) Gary Hamel, Yves L. Doz and C.K.Prahlad, Collaborate with your competitors and win **Harvard Business Review on Strategic Alliance**

62) Michael E. Porter, The competitive advantage of nations **Free Press**

63) Angel Robert (2003), A new dawn in CRM: This time it is B2B, **Ivey Business Journal**.,July-August.

64) Brown Stanley A. and Moosha Gulycz, (2002), Performance driven CRM, PWC Consulting, John- Wilcy .

65) Gordon Ian (2002), Best Practices: Customer Relationship management, **Ivey Business Jr.**, Nov-Dec.

66) David Walters and Geoff Lancaster (2000), Implementing value strategy through the value chain, **MCB University Press.**161-177

67) David Walters and Mark Rainbird (2004), The demand chain as an integral component of the value chain, **Journal of Consumer Marketing.**466-472

68) Goran Svensson (2003), Consumer driven and bi-directional value chain diffusion models, **European Business Review.**391-396

69) David H.Taylor (2005), Value chain analysis: an approach to supply chain improvement in agri-food chains**, International Journal of Physical Distribution & Logistics Management.**747-749

70) Mark Rainbird (2004), A framework for operations management: the value chain, **International Journal of Physical Distribution& Logistics Management**.340-345

71) Clark Eustace (2003), A new perspective on the knowledge of value chain, **Journal of Intellectual Capital.**591-593

72) Ganesh D.Bhatt and Ali F.Emdad (2001), An analysis of the virtual value chain in electronic commerce, **MCB University Press**.79-83

73) Yildirim Yilmaz and Umit Bititci(2005), Performance measurement in the value chain: manufacturing V.tourism, **International Journal of Productivity and Performance Management** 373-381

74) Oswald A.Mascarenhas, ram Kesavan and Michael Bernacchi (2004), Customer value-chain involvement for co-creating customer delight, **Journal of Consumer Marketing.** 486-491

75) David Bovet and Joseph Martha (2000), Value nets: reinventing the rusty supply chain for competitive advantage, **John Wiley & Sons**. 21-26

76) David Walters and Mark Rainbird(2007), Cooperative innovation: a value chain approach, **Journal of Enterprise Information Management**.599-606

77) David W.Crain and Stan Abraham (2006), Using value-chain analysis to discover customers strategic needs, **Strategy & leadership.** 29-37

78) Prescott C. Ensign (1998), Interrelationships and horizontal strategy to achieve synergy and competitive advantage in the diversified firm, **MCB University Press**.657-665

79) G.Ian Burke and Denise G.Farratt(2004), The influence of information and advice on competitive strategy definition in small and medium sized enterprises, **Qualitative Market Research: An international journal**. 129-135

80) John A.Parnell (2006), Generic strategies after two decades: a reconceptualization of competitive strategy, **Management Decision**.1145-1147

81) Nuran Acur and Frank Gertsen, Hongyi Sun and Jan Frick (2003), The formalization of manufacturing strategy and its influence on the relationship between competitive objectives, improvement goals, and action plans, **International Journal of Operations & production management**.1115-1121

82) William A.Drago (1996), Strategic Plan Intensity and competitive strategy, **Management research news.** 13-17

83) John Thompson (1995), Strategic and competitive success: towards a model of the comprehensively competent organization, **MCB University Press**. 5-15

84) Uta Juttner and Hans Peter Wehrli (1994), Competitive Advantage: Merging marketing and the Competence-based Perspective, **Journal of Business & Industrial marketing**. 44-48

85) **Certain assessment & ideas from MIT World video releases environment & energy for the last chapter (chapter11)**